Cohesion and Collusion:

Promoting the 2003 Invasion of Iraq

Under way, the new skipper,
first mate, and other officers,
charged with maintaining good
order and discipline, did invite
zealous civilian subordinates to
the helm to join with them in
directing the ship of state.
Perversely excited in charting
together a course to safety,
they put the great vessel upon
the rocks.

Cohesion and Collusion:

Promoting the 2003 Invasion of Iraq

HAROLD BARRETT

Parkerson Publishing

An imprint of Parkerson Publishing

COHESION AND COLLUSION: PROMOTING THE 2003 INVASION OF IRAQ

By Harold Barrett

ISBN 9781796373806

Mara J. Lavery, proofreader and indexer—Cover design by Roselise

Realism vs. idealism—Dick Cheney and nationalism—Neoconservatism as persuasion—cohesion and consubstantiality—invasion of Iraq—US foreign policy—George W. Bush and White House force

United States of America, June 2019

In our family, we enjoy helping. Wende is a huge example. Son Joe, a ready helper, says it's no big deal, explaining simply, "It's what we do."

A la familia que cuida—¡gracias a todos!

Acknowledgments

Eric Alterman, in one of his worthy, plain-speaking essays, concluded with a fervent exhortation on conducting open investigations: "Let there be light," he pleaded. A gratifying number of writers whom I consulted conformed to this injunction and thus offered support of my work: e.g., Michael Massing, Joshua Micah Marshall, Michael Isikoff, David Corn, Stephen M. Walt and colleague John J. Mearsheimer, and Jason Vest. Good citizens, all.

The reliable reporting and analyses of *The Guardian* newspaper were valuable to me. Kudos to Brian Whitaker and his colleagues: Peter Bergen, Julian Borger, Trevor Timm, and all others.

I hope that Jim Lobe and Seymour Hersh will accept stars of excellence for their unselfish service in informing an unknowing public: for their bringing vital political activity to a visible level.

I am also indebted to contributions of Craig Unger, Juan Cole, Thomas E. Ricks, James Bamford, Janine R. Wedel, and Andrew

Bacevich. These writers deserve our notice, dedicated as they are to conveying relevant and important knowledge.

The historical and biographical book of Jacob Heilbrunn was of the highest order, refreshingly welcome in its breadth of coverage, generosity, and obvious intellectual independence. I thank him for *They Knew They Were Right,* a work of maturity. I have not read a better one in my investigation.

Wende Kim, Edward Paul, Kelsey Lynn, Patti Walker, Wilson Reed, Umberto, Jacob Scott, and Joe George served the author many times and many ways. Truly indispensable they were.

Roselise designed the cover and, with Sue Mainwaring's support, produced a harmonious and decorous product.

Colleagues Millard and Ruth Petersky, Ginny Hennes, Sandy Wiatr, and Chuck Eck contributed skillfully and unselfishly as manuscript readers. Barbara Royal graciously lent a hand.

Professors Gerry Philipsen and Leah Ceccarelli were there with good advice at critical times.

Thanks to historian Dick Kirkendall, who along the way kindly but bluntly said, "No, not yet," when I asked if I had established the thesis.

The author deeply appreciates the decades of wisdom and guidance provided by Charles M. Guss, John M. Fanucchi, Orvell K. Fletcher, Earl F. Osborn, Wendell Holmes Stephenson, Bower Aly, Roy C. McCall, Robert D. Clark, Roderick P. Hart, and Kenneth Burke. And let me reach way back and add another name: Mrs. Irene Long, at Healdsburg High School, who taught us to appreciate the English sentence.

And speaking of the past, this time to a man whose name is rarely seen in a book's acknowledgment section. He is a famous scholar of ancient Athens, the one who lectured on rhetoric (and, oh yes, on some other subjects) while strolling the *peripatos* of the Lyceum: Aristotle walked and talked, while his walking and learning listeners took notes. Let's acknowledge them, too! Both deserve our gratitude.

Mara J. Lavery, a professional reader, is an artist and super sleuth who contributed admirably to the metamorphosis of a promising manuscript becoming a good book. Also, readers will appreciate her construction of a comprehensive, useful index.

My Carol is not here to help this time. She and I read proof together thirteen times from the '50s on. There was love in that labor. We knew the meaning of love—in all things.

Contents

Overview   1

1   *A Glance Back*   5

2   *Profiles of Neoconservatives*   19

3   *Think Tanks*   60

4   *Chalabi*   75

5   *Managing Perceptions*   83

6   *Writers*   91

7   *Two Eventful Decades*   113

8   *The White House*   127

9   *Al-Qaeda Attacked the US*   164

10 *The Office of Special Plans*   178

11 *Cohesion*   186

12 *The Invasion*   194

13 *Reporting to the People*   206

14 *Provenance of a Disaster*   212

Works Consulted   215

Appendix   271

Index   287

About the Author   311

Overview

A memorable event occurred in 2015. At dinner with friends, the name "Paul Wolfowitz" came up. Someone called him "an evil guy." Dick, a well-known historian, stiffened a bit and asked, "Evil?"

We abandoned the topic, but I remembered that moment and decided to do some personal fact-checking on the subject. Caught up in reading from the plethora of relevant material available, I found myself deep in a study of the so-called neoconservatives and their historical beginnings, goals, effectiveness, and so forth. The results of my exciting investigation go well beyond a simple follow-up to a dinner-time conversation. Forty years ago, as an aspiring scholar in rhetoric, I had written one dissertation. Here is another, this one titled, *Cohesion and Collusion.*

The neoconservative part of the story begins with young Jewish men, students at the University of Chicago finding inspiration in association with philosopher Professor Leo Strauss. Paul Wolfowitz was one of them. Others had studied at major universities, principally Harvard and Yale. For several, a critical turning point occurred in the 1970s when they came under the influence of Albert J. Wohlstetter and US Senator Henry M. Jackson. Thanks to these estimable gentlemen, these young neocons found places to work and, like their mentors, became people of influence.

Coming after neoconservative pioneer Irving Kristol, they observed extant US foreign policy, seeing unmet ugly forces in the world that constituted a threat to good nations. The neocons came to advocate that American democracy be installed across the globe and, if necessary, by military might and preemptive attack. The weak US military must be strengthened to the point of clear domination over all others. Focusing attention on the Middle East, they asserted that Saddam Hussein of Iraq was a builder of weapons of mass destruction and had to be removed, and Israel, a valued and vulnerable sister of the US, secured. The attacks of September 11, 2001, intensified the fever sharply.

Ensuing chapters highlight unfailing strategies used by neoconservatives to promote an invasion of Iraq: uses of think tanks, the creation of their own effective intelligence apparatus, preparation of prescriptive defense documents, and use of public relations methods for promotion of an invasion of Iraq.

Then, at the turn of the century, a second unit of persuasion was growing. Texas governor George Walker Bush, son of a former US president, entered the US political scene. He, too, had a gnawing and rich heritage and a desire to advance. Republicans set up a program to help him learn things that every president needed to know. Clearly aware of his deficiencies, Bush was a willing trainee. Richard Cheney became his running mate.

Soon after their coming together as candidates, Bush and Dick Cheney discussed a sharing of presidential obligations and began to communicate on the topic. They were elected in 2000, and together, given Cheney's notable political savvy and Bush's need, they made it work.

Needing a supportive voice in the White House, Cheney called up his long-time associate Donald Rumsfeld to be defense secretary. Cheney's power steadily grew.

With the persistently persuasive presence of Vice President Dick Cheney, the White House leadership became a unified nationalist triad favoring action against Iraq. On March 19, 2003, the US attacked Iraq, effected by the cohesive neoconservative persuasion and the cohesive Bush-Cheney-Rumsfeld force. Let's focus in on details.

Details follow.

1

A Glance Back

Formation of a Goal

Activities of the neoconservatives grew from their forbears' passions in the 1930s and '40s. Predecessors were committed Trotskyite communist intellectuals and combative anti-Stalinists. The Cold War began in the late '40s, and as anticommunist partisans, neoconservatives railed against the misdirection of the Soviet revolution. The Cold War lasted for forty years.

With victory over the Soviets, these conservative belligerents found a home in the Republican Party, where ordinarily they were welcomed, yes, but the regulars were of a different conservative stripe.

These young, aggressive, intellectual right wingers were drawn to another vision. They were *neo* conservatives. They would not suffer the likes of ordinary conservatives, e.g., G.H.W.

Bush, Jim Baker, and Brent Scowcroft, so-called *realists* in government. Realists were politicians who sought détente and *containment* of rival nations, choosing to use ordinary diplomacy, working with nations *multilaterally,* talking it over. Often, they hammered out small gains in the international give-and-take of reconciling clashes and moving forward. The realists accepted the regimen of steady, often tedious and hard, artful diplomatic work.

But not the new type: they were convinced that good nations face evil all around; therefore, the United States must "not be ashamed to use its unrivaled power—forcefully if necessary—to promote its values around the world." Old methods in international relations are weak. Threats "can no longer be reliably contained and therefore must be prevented, sometimes through preemptive military action." Neocons "even speak of the need to cultivate a US empire" ("Neocon 101"). Yes, they assured their audiences, the US will fight—alone, if necessary.

Joshua Muravchik, a reliable spokesperson, authoritatively provides an overview of the emergence of this neoconservative perspective, calling for development of US superiority to "fashion a benign world order" (Muravchik). Realism is useless against terrorism, he and colleagues proclaimed; it is merely standing still, not moving ahead, yielding the lead to other nations of the world. Any form of "containment" is like treading water. It is weak. Only unmistakable military power is understood.

At work in and out of government, the neoconservatives held fast in their goal of furthering the use of the armed forces of the United States to further democracy in the Middle East, preemptively subduing enemies and building an indomitable presence in the region.

In any account of the beginnings of neoconservative political strength in the United States, certain names stand out: Leo Strauss, Albert J. Wohlstetter, United States Senator Henry M. Jackson, and Irving Kristol.

Leo Strauss, 1899–1973

German-born Leo Strauss was the "inspirational founder of American neoconservatism" (Sheppard 1) and one whose work is often credited as providing a philosophical and motivational underpinning.

In his youth in Europe, Strauss became a Zionist. Brandeis's Eugene Sheppard writes insightfully that Strauss "sought to reconcile the conflicts of a Jew unwilling to surrender loyalty to his ancestral community" (Sheppard 1). Strauss has been named the fundamental force behind the "goal of democratizing the Middle East through military force." While controversial, he had "intensely loyal followers who proudly described themselves as 'Straussians'" (Linker). As young "Straussians" moved to places in the political world, their influence widened, and their radiance attracted others; the fever spread. Though many neocons demonstrated the influence of Leo Strauss, a minority can be called "Straussians."

Shadia B. Drury, while an earnest critic of the work of Leo Strauss, does find him to be an "important philosopher worthy of careful study and criticism. He is a philosopher in the rich and meaningful sense of having a most comprehensive view of the world: of life and death, morality and religion, politics and society, justice and injustice." And he "forces us to look into the dark depths of our *psyches;* like Machiavelli, he forces us to come to terms with the nastiness of politics." But, she attests, Strauss corrupts. He "seduces young men into thinking that they belong to a special and privileged class of individuals that transcend ordinary humanity and the rules applicable to other people" (Drury 4, 93).

Yes, as a sophisticated European and Jew, Strauss did recognize threatening world conditions; he experienced periods of fascism in Germany for the first half of his life. America offered hope. With him in his classes at the University of Chicago were smart, strong men who were ready to stand up and were open to moving toward commitment against the existing evils. One acquainted with the professor's yearning heart can comfortably substitute the word "captivate" or "charm" for Drury's word "seduce" and thereby put a more positive light on Strauss's interaction with his Chicago students. Strauss did, indeed, ask his students to recognize and make use of their elitism. They were special, becoming equipped to take arms against worldly wrongs.

In 2006, Leo Strauss's 1956 letter to the editors of the *National Review* was republished as "Leo Strauss's Traditionalist Defense of Israel." He wrote the letter to show resentment for the magazine's unqualified and "incomprehensible" opposition to the state of

Israel. Strauss reminded readers that Israel is a "Western country, which educates its many immigrants from the East in the ways of the West: Israel is the only country which stands as an outpost of the West in the East." Moreover, Israel is "surrounded by mortal enemies." Surely, no country is as heroically austere and less lethargic, he observed (Auster). The welfare of Israel is an issue in all credible reports on the beginnings and motivations of neoconservatism.

In addition to acknowledging elitism as necessary to successful leadership and recognizing Israel's value to the West, this professor of the classics argues with great disdain against historicism. Adherents of that perspective advance "the claim that all values, ideologies, and regimes are historically relative to time and place," defining it as a fraudulent attempt "to justify injustice and inequality." The historicist notes changes in the unfolding of generations, thereby becoming unable to distinguish right from wrong, leading adherents to seek temporal respect and honors, success in their time. "The typical historicism of the twentieth century demands that each generation reinterpret the past on the basis of its own experience and with a view to its own future. It is no longer contemplative, but activistic"; no

"objective norms remained" (Strauss 17, 59).
Strauss affirmed that the wisdom of ancient
thinkers has relevance today—and will
tomorrow.

Such is the bewitching and emancipating
character of Straussian influence on the
formation of neoconservative ideology,
particularly in regard to foreign policy.

Albert J. Wohlstetter, 1913–1997

Wohlstetter, friend of Leo Strauss, is another
great figure in the forming of neoconservative
thought and spirit. He was a prime disseminator
of Straussian values. He too enjoys deity status
in the history, often given the appellation,
"neoconservative godfather." Trained as logician
and mathematician, he joined the faculty of the
University of Chicago in 1964 and became
closely associated with Professor Strauss.

Before Chicago, from 1951 to 1963,
Wohlstetter was a senior policy analyst at the
Rand Corporation, specializing in military
technology, particularly nuclear strategy. He
returned to Rand in later years. Enthralled with
game theory and the use of statistical models of
national defense, he and his colleague, wife
Roberta, were relentless and staunch advocates

of military preparation—readiness for all eventualities. Full national security was their declared goal, one to be achieved at any cost.

Always forthright and controversial, during the Cold War the Wohlstetters developed and presented detailed systems of defense strategies with great vigor. Albert Wohlstetter "argued that nuclear deterrence wasn't sufficient—the US had to actually plan to fight a nuclear war in order to deter it" (Drew).

The words of Khurram Husain, author for the *Bulletin for the Atomic Scientists,* capture an essence of the mind-set of Albert Wohlstetter and his "iron law of zero margin of error." Wohlstetter proclaimed, even a "small probability of vulnerability, or potential future vulnerability could be presented as a virtual state of national emergency" (Husain). Jude Wanniski, a former colleague of Albert Wohlstetter, remembered his hawkish view on military preemption against probable enemies: if "you look down the road and see a war with, say China, twenty years off, go to war now" (Pace). There is no more concise way to define preemption.

Wohlstetter was a magnet to dialogue and participated brilliantly, attracting others, always widening his circle. Much to his enjoyment, he typically was the center of attention—on any occasion. For instance, intellectuals, young and of kindred enthusiasm, formed around him. He was for them an indefatigable, gifted, natty and sophisticated, up-to-the-minute, and self-assured model. Keen and ever prepared, Wohlstetter opened doors for his acolytes, "calling the shots," and seeing that they found the right places to function effectively. He was adept at selecting people for given roles and placing them strategically. He felt responsible.

"Thanks in large part to Wohlstetter, to his methodology, his demeanor, his political know-how, protoneocons learned how to turn their ideas into political action" (Unger, *Fall* 42).

Colleagues and acquaintances pointed to his display of ego. "He was almost totally consumed with himself—very narcissistic," says Leonard Binder, a fellow professor at the University of Chicago (Swidey). To be sure, Albert Wohlstetter was an outstanding man, in a number of senses; he thrived on status, on being No. 1.

Senator Henry M. Jackson, 1912–1983

Born in Everett, Washington, of Norwegian immigrants, Henry M. "Scoop" Jackson served in the United States Senate for the last thirty years of his life, to 1983. (Incidentally, his fond sister decided to call him "Scoop" after a comic character of their day. Others picked it up, and it stuck.) Politically, he was a Democrat, a liberal who supported social welfare, civil rights, labor unions, and environmental protection. But on national defense, he was a rigid conservative. In the US Senate, Jackson was an ardent hawk, known for exerting legislative acumen in building national defenses, always.

Albert Wohlstetter esteemed Jackson's proclivities, and he, too, was ever on the lookout for ways to increase US power. Wohlstetter saw to it that certain of his and Leo Strauss's most promising stalwarts—all Jewish, young, and eager to go at it—went to work with Senator Jackson. Wohlstetter arranged their entry to the "Bunker," as the senator's office was called. Starting in 1969, Wohlstetter's strategic posting of neoconservatives to Senator Jackson's office added significantly to the mounting of US power against Soviet aggression. Paternalistic Jackson "engendered fierce loyalty." He and his initiates shared a secular "version of American exceptionalism"; knowing America as the savior nation, they were bent on eliminating communism (Unger, *Fall* 38).

To be sure, the young zealots were in an advantageous position, close to a fatherly and enthusiastic United States senator and close to the action in the Department of Defense. Thanks to Dr. Wohlstetter's will and the senator's welcome and compatible political orientation, these nascent neocons found support and a hospitable environment for shaping their careers. Jackson's political philosophy influenced them; doubtless the influencing was mutual. Neoconservatives who worked with Senator Jackson in the Bunker included Paul Wolfowitz and Richard Perle, Elliott Abrams, Abram Shulsky, Zalmay Khalilzad, Joshua Muravchik, Frank Gaffney, and Douglas Feith, among others. All would become big figures in enhancing the military promise of the US. Jackson, in turn, was a trusted mentor and adviser, actively promoting the individual careers and ambitions of his staff (University of Washington). Ahead, we will meet a number of these important neoconservative figures.

Senator Jackson maintained a close and always favorable relationship with Israel and its leaders. In the early '70s he added luster to his bearing, not to mention increasing his popularity among many, by cosponsoring an amendment to a Senate Soviet trade bill that allowed thousands of Russian Jews to migrate freely to the United States (Kampeas). By the 1970s "Jackson was the leading Congressional supporter of increased military aid to Israel" (Oldham). In 2002, reporter Jason Vest looked back and designated Scoop Jackson "the Senate's most zealous champion of Israel in his day" (Vest).

Senator Jackson died 20 years before the invasion of Iraq.

Each year, the Jewish Institute for National Security Affairs (JINSA) confers their Distinguished Service Award on a person whose career has demonstrated zeal in supporting a strong US military capability. The first recipient in 1982 was Senator Jackson. Then, in further remembrance of a dear friend, the award, after his death, was renamed the Senator Henry M. "Scoop" Jackson Distinguished Service Award. Above all others, he had contributed to US national security. Among winners in subsequent years were Max Cleland, Joe Lieberman, Dick

Cheney, Jane Harman, and Paul Wolfowitz ("History").

Irving Kristol, 1920–2009

Irving Kristol has been named the founding father of neoconservatism. He called neoconservatism a *persuasion,* a characterization that this study of rhetorical interaction finds fitting. Kristol believed that neoconservatism serves as a counterforce to political realism—to realpolitik, the long-time Republican strategy in foreign policy. He—and we can add **Norman Podhoretz**—stand as preparers of the substantial ground from which neoconservatism grew. Podhoretz edited the *Commentary* magazine for 35 years, between 1960 and 1995. Unilateral theory in foreign affairs was a common subject advanced in his magazine.

Irving Kristol wrote steadily from the '40s on. Along the way, he founded numerous political magazines. He and **Daniel Bell** brought out *The Public Interest* in 1965, where he spent most of his publishing life. The magazine stopped publishing in 2005. His bimonthly magazine, *The National Interest*, appeared in 1985. He and **Stephen Spender** founded

Encounter magazine in 1953. He was editor of the anticommunist magazine *The Reporter* for a brief period in the late '50s.

Kristol gave space in his magazines to these brilliant neocons who offered the world challenging ideas: confronting Soviet ambitions and warning Americans of impotence in the United States' defense establishment. These *new* conservatives urged strategic conquest of threatening countries—while seeking the security and prosperity of Israel, a condition that became quite clear in this study.

In the 1970s, Irving Kristol switched his political identity, joining the Republican Party. The new conservatives, the sophisticated legatees, were quick out of the blocks. In declaiming their theory of national defense, they adopted and skillfully executed Irving Kristol's idea of persuasion.

2

Profiles of Neoconservatives

Two Prominent Neoconservatives

Always observed as two of the most accomplished neoconservative leaders are Paul D. Wolfowitz and Richard N. Perle.

Paul D. Wolfowitz was born in Brooklyn, NY, in 1943, the son of a Polish immigrant father whose family died in the Holocaust. In 1965, he earned a BA in mathematics at Cornell University and became a student of Leo Strauss at the University of Chicago. In 1972, under Albert Wohlstetter, he earned a PhD at the University of Chicago; his dissertation was on nuclear proliferation in the Middle East.

Wolfowitz's experience is varied and extensive. He joined Senator Henry M. Jackson's staff in 1973 and worked in the Department of Defense (or DoD) with the Arms Control and Disarmament Agency, leaving in 1977; under President Jimmy Carter, from 1977 to 1980 he was deputy assistant secretary of defense for regional programs; and then under President Reagan, from 1981 to 1982 he served as head of the policy planning staff at the State Department. From 1983 to1986, he held the post of assistant secretary of state for the Bureau of East Asian and Pacific Affairs; he served as the United States ambassador to Indonesia from 1986 to1989, where he had an immediate opportunity to learn of a Muslim culture.

From 1989 to1993, with President George H.W. Bush, he was back in the DoD, as undersecretary, at the time of the Persian Gulf War. In 1993, he taught at the National War College at National Defense University, before becoming dean of the School of Advanced International Studies at Johns Hopkins University from 1994 to 2001, even while he continued to promote a policy of defense expansion, a chief career activity.

Wolfowitz and his mentor, Albert Wohlstetter, became fast political companions. Richard Perle once said, "Paul thinks the way Albert thinks" (Bacevich).

Dick Cheney, vice president to George W. Bush, saw to it that Wolfowitz was named deputy secretary in the DoD (Unger, "Cheney"), subordinate only to Secretary Rumsfeld.

The deputy secretary, the second-highest ranking official in the DoD, is delegated full power and authority to act for the secretary and to exercise the powers of the secretary on any and all matters for which the secretary is authorized to act (DoD, "About").

This position was the highest attained by Wolfowitz in his productive political career.

In an interview on the Public Broadcasting System's *News Hour,* three days after the 9/11 air attack on the US, the viewers saw a composed and resolute Deputy Secretary of Defense Paul Wolfowitz speak urgently for a quick and telling response to the surprise incident (Warner). His effort to effect an invasion of Iraq was unrelenting from that point on.

Interestingly, in his advocacy of war, Paul Wolfowitz revealed an idealism—and pragmatism: if democracy were to endure and democracy prosper, the US must create strategies of military defense against the everthreating behavior of evil nations. This was the major premise of his reasoning on the need for war.

He spent decades in government working continuously to maintain the security of the US and allies. Paul Wolfowitz was a hawk and an ideological leader in promoting a preemptive attack against Saddam Hussein, the hated dictator in Iraq. Wolfowitz is often referred to as the principal "architect" of the invasion of Iraq.

Richard N. Perle was born in 1941 in New York City. He earned a BA in English at the University of Southern California in 1964 and an MA in political science at Princeton University in 1967. As an undergraduate, he studied at the London School of Economics and the International Study Program in Denmark.

When a student at Hollywood High School, Perle was a classmate of Hollywood stars and, eventfully, Joan Wohlstetter. She sat next to him in Spanish and invited him over to swim. One day at the pool, young Perle met Joan's father, Albert Wohlstetter, the bright political thinker. He became Perle's friend, counselor, colleague, and fellow strategist. At poolside that day, Wohlstetter brought out a copy of his remarkable paper, "Delicate Balance of Terror," an authoritative and powerful essay—and very readable—detailing thermonuclear dangers inherent in the strategic relationship between the United States and the Soviet Union (Wohlstetter). Perle read the article straightaway, and the two talked about it. The Wohlstetter article became widely known as a brilliant statement on foreign affairs (Wattenberg). Perle's appreciation of the piece was unbounded: "What I liked about it was how rigorous the argument was. It was just very elegant, systematic, and orderly...beautifully argued" (Weisman 19).

Richard Perle began his political career as a senior staff member to Senator Henry M. Jackson, working on the Senate Armed Services Committee. He recalled the day he got the call from Albert Wohlstetter in 1969: he "phoned me....Could you come to Washington for a few days and interview some people...on the current debate shaping up in the Senate over ballistic missile defense.... I've asked somebody else .... too [Paul Wolfowitz], and maybe you could work together" (Wattenberg). And, fatefully, the two did work together. Perle stayed with Senator Jackson until 1980.

Meeting Scoop Jackson, Perle reports, was a case of "love at first sight....I was there for eleven years" ("Richard Perle-biography"). They worked in the Bunker together, those tough, uncompromising souls, dedicated to overhauling the US defense system. We shall meet some of Perle's diligent neoconservative colleagues at later points in this book.

Perle assumed other political roles, among them assistant defense secretary in arms control from 1981 to 1987 in the Reagan presidency, this being his only official assignment in government. Also, much more notably, he was a member of the important Defense Policy Advisory Board Committee from 1987 to 2004, during the presidencies of Ronald Reagan, G.H.W. Bush, Bill Clinton, and G.W. Bush.

In 2001, George W. Bush appointed Richard Perle chairman of that influential board, a very desirable position given the available business opportunities. The role of board members—the thirty or so former government officials, retired military officers, and academics—is to advise the DoD secretary on perceived needs and offer him feedback on their observations.

Significantly, many on the board, like Perle, had business contracts with the Pentagon. Membership was coveted. During Perle's chairmanship, the Board's budget and power grew. The charter—administered in the DoD—specifies that the

> Defense Policy Board will serve the public interest by providing the Secretary of Defense, Deputy Secretary of Defense and the Under Secretary of Defense for Policy with independent, informed advice and opinion concerning major matters of defense policy. It will focus upon long-term, enduring issues central to strategic planning for the Department of Defense and will be responsible for research and analysis of topics, long or short range, addressed to it by the Secretary of Defense, Deputy Secretary of Defense and the Under Secretary of Defense for Policy. (United States Defense Policy Board)

Perle had many enviable business involvements, including senior adviser to the Monitor Group (specialists in financial planning and investment); cochairman of Hollinger International (a holding company, owned by the *Jerusalem Post*); managing partner with Trireme

Partners (venture capital company investing in technology, goods, and services related to homeland security); consultant to Global Crossings, a telecommunications corporation; cochairman for Morgan Crucible (world's larger supplier of nonferrous crucibles); director of *Jerusalem Post;* and many more.

Some of his dealings in the realms of trade had political dimensions and led to complications and accusations—for instance, in Perle's business exchanges with Israelis. He was accused in 1983, when serving as assistant secretary of defense, of recommending to the army that it buy certain weapons from an Israeli company from which he had accepted a consulting fee. *New York Times* reporter Jeff Gerth has laid out details of this and other alleged breaches (Gerth).

More serious is an instance of a conflict that arose when, while serving as chairman of the Defense Policy Advisory Board Committee, Perle represented a business that had filed contracts with the Department of Defense. He was a partner in Trireme, a company expecting handsome profits if war with Iraq were to occur. He was a war advocate and saddled with a serious charge of impropriety. The accusation

drew much attention in the press. Writer
Seymour Hersh's magazine article on the activity
was forthright. Hersh noted, "One of the general
rules is that you don't take advantage of your
federal position to help yourself financially in
any way" (Hersh, "Lunch"). Perle was forced to
resign his chairmanship, which was a very big
loss for him, both economically and morally.

In another case, an "FBI summary of a
1970 wiretap recorded Perle discussing
classified information with someone at the
Israeli embassy." When the case became
wrapped up in a political snarl, National
Security Advisor Henry Kissinger stepped in with
an explanation, and Perle was exonerated
(Hersh, "Kissinger").

Perle was omnipresent in the media,
always in the political or business limelight.
Politically, he was ever ready with a message for
America, usually an ominous warning about this
nation's defensive incapacity against a network
of enemies who, he reported, would soon be
confronting the nation with nuclear weapons.
His visage was grim and his message dire as he
was interviewed on CNN, appearing on *Frontline*
or in print on pages of the *Weekly Standard,* the
New Republic, or other newspapers or

magazines. He loved to argue and was smooth and convincing in conveying his dreadful tidings. In a CNN interview five days after 9/11, now available on *YouTube,* he claimed, "Yes, we know that Osama bin Laden has ties with Saddam Hussein...that can be documented" (CNN, "Richard Perle - The Next Attack").

That assertion was patently false. Again, in January 2003, two months before the invasion of Iraq, he arranged an interview with *Frontline,* and while seeming to respond to all queries deftly, some viewers saw him as weak in evidence to back his grand generalizations. As always, he rejected a multilateral approach in dealing with Iraq, disdaining a realist resolution (Perle, "Closed Doors").

Richard Perle's multifaceted countenance is a marvelous model of an ever-occupied and diversified operator with a bulging political and business schedule. He took advantage of opportunities, jumping from one deal to another, exploiting a chance to turn the heads of listeners or readers, articulately and solemnly arguing for or against some measure from his peculiar perch. He was a steady source of material to the media, speaking or writing in his dark demeanor. In a sketch, Sydney Blumenthal provides an emphatic picture of Perle's wheeling and dealings. "He was exceedingly smooth, exceedingly articulate, and exceedingly disarming" (Blumenthal).

We might take these two neoconservative advocates, Wolfowitz and Perle, as Mr. Inside and Mr. Outside. Paul Wolfowitz, in his position of power *inside* the Bush administration, answered the September 11 attack by conceptualizing and constructing a case for war. Richard Perle was a figure *outside* government (except for his critical participation on the Defense Policy Advisory Board Committee), in the country talking and writing in his matchless style while arguing his case in all quarters—he the persevering whiz of all venues. The following six neocons were also in the first tier of achievement.

Other Accomplished Neoconservatives

We will now meet six other powerful neoconservatives, all colleagues of Paul Wolfowitz and Richard Perle, many of them active in government positions. Their profiles serve to show a variety in unity among members of this conservative corps: in their general conduct, approaches to issues, and strategies.

Withal, their substantial core and driving purpose held fast. As we move along randomly with brief sketches, their contrasting characterizations and persistent drive toward a single goal will become apparent.

Elliott Abrams was born in 1948; he graduated from Harvard College in 1969 and then earned an MA in International Relations at the London School of Economics in 1970 and a JD from Harvard Law School in 1973.

He was a diplomat, lawyer, and politician with an abiding interest in foreign policy.

After assisting Senator Jackson in his 1972 campaign for president, Abrams stayed on to work in Jackson's office until 1976. He was chief of staff / special counsel for Sen. Daniel P. Moynihan from 1977 to 1979. He held three positions under President Ronald Reagan: assistant secretary of state for International Organization Affairs, 1981; assistant secretary of state for Democracy, Human Rights, and Labor, 1981 to 1985; and assistant secretary of state for Western Hemisphere Affairs, 1985 to 1989. Abrams also advised in the administration of President George W. Bush. He was special assistant to the president and senior director of

the National Security Council for Democracy,
Human Rights, and International Organizations
from 2001 to 2002 and for Near East and North
African Affairs from 2002 to 2005, after which
he served as deputy assistant to the president
and deputy national security advisor for global
democracy strategy.

Abrams was extraordinarily active in many
think tanks and other political organizations,
e.g., Council on Foreign Relations, Middle
Eastern Studies, Project for the New American
Century (or PNAC), American Jewish Committee,
Heritage Foundation, Committee on US Interests
in the Middle East, and Hudson Institute.

Elliott Abrams was "hell bent" to give his
all for the cause, as evidenced in his vigorous
support for the contras of Nicaragua.
Incidentally, from that challenging experience,
he came to believe that to be effective in
government, one must "stay behind the scenes
and keep out of the headlines" (Heilbrunn 184).
But not always, it seems, did he follow that
course (Alterman, "Rehabilitation").

His fiery political essays appeared in
Commentary, Weekly Standard, and other
publications. Craig Unger characterized him as a

"staunch, take-no-prisoners hard-liner" (Unger, *Fall* 204), and to David Corn he was "as nasty a policy warrior as Washington had seen in decades" (Corn, "Elliott Abrams").

Indeed, he was uncommonly outspoken and aggressive in advocacy of the intervention by the United States in the Middle East, unswerving in attention to the welfare of Israel; also, he promoted a strongly pro-Israel stance toward peace negotiations with the Palestinians, criticizing the 1993 Oslo Accords as "too demanding of Israel" (Crowley).

He wrote a number of books on foreign policy and three on the Jewish faith and spirituality.

Elliott Abrams fought hard and opened his heart to the world: "Outside the land of Israel, there can be no doubt that Jews, faithful to the covenant between God and Abraham, are to stand apart from the nation in which they live." He implored that

> this should not imply disloyalty to America
> or any other country where Jews live
> outside of Israel, but that Jews must be
> loyal to Israel because they are in a
> permanent covenant with God and with

the land of Israel and its people. ("Elliott Abrams," *Jewish Virtual Library*)

His position on maintaining a bond with Israel is akin to that of Professor Leo Strauss.

It was discovered that, in the congressional debate on the Iran-Contra affair, he had withheld information. He was sentenced to two years' probation and required to complete one hundred hours of community service. President George H.W. Bush granted Abrams a pardon in 1992 (Brown).

Douglas Feith was born in 1953. He earned an AB from Harvard University in 1975 and a JD from Georgetown University in 1978.

It is notable that at Harvard he studied under Richard Pipes, thirty years his senior and father of neocon Daniel Pipes, perhaps experiencing the spirit of the former generation of pioneer neoconservatives.

Feith practiced law, once heading his own law firm. In 1975 he joined the staff of Senator Jackson, staying until deciding to help Admiral Zumwalt in his unsuccessful run for the United States Senate in 1976. He taught briefly at Georgetown University and Stanford University.

During the first Reagan administration, Feith was on the National Security Council staff as Middle East analyst, but in 1981 Richard Perle led him to the Department of Defense as a special counsel. In 1984 Secretary Caspar Weinberger elevated him to deputy assistant secretary of defense and in 1986 presented him with the highest DoD civilian award: the Department of Defense Medal for Distinguished Public Service.

In 2001, Feith was appointed undersecretary of defense for policy in the Bush administration, joining his comrade Paul Wolfowitz, who was No. 2 in the DoD. Thus, Feith became No. 3, occupying a strategic position in working directly with Secretary Donald Rumsfeld.

He wrote a big book in 2008, *War and Decision*, on various aspects of the invasion and occupation of Iraq. It is needy of verification on a number of points—"truth checking"—but regarding the book, the well-known intellectual Christopher Hitchens advised, "If you want to read a serious book about the intervention in Iraq, look to Douglas Feith" (Hitchens).

When Feith left the NSC to become deputy assistant secretary of defense, he was soon promoted. But that was before it was discovered that he had left the NSC involuntarily. He had been fired after the FBI found him to be a suspect in showing confidential documents to an Israeli embassy official. The case was dropped, and Feith carried on.

Douglas Feith was one of the most politically active of all neoconservatives. A major effort was his key part in implementing the Office of Special Plans (OSP), a vital mechanism in the run-up to the invasion of Iraq. I will introduce the OSP and discuss Feith's function at a later point.

John Bolton was born in 1948; he graduated from Yale University with a BA degree in 1970 and earned a JD in 1974.

Bolton is a lawyer, diplomat, politician, and a member of the National Rifle Association. He holds membership in the Council for National Policy, an ultraconservative private club that meets behind closed doors three or four times a year. Among its membership were Pat Robertson, Ed Meese, John Ashcroft, Col. Oliver

North, Jerry Falwell, Betsy Devos, and Richard Viguerie.

Bolton served actively in various positions during the administrations of Ronald Reagan, G.H.W. Bush, and G.W. Bush. He was general counsel to the United States Agency for International Development (USAID) from 1981 to 1982. This agency attacked extreme poverty in democratic countries, helping them to grow as nations. He served as USAID's assistant administrator for program and policy coordination from 1982 to 1983; he was assistant attorney general in the Department of Justice from 1985 to 1989 and assistant secretary for the Bureau of International Organization Affairs at the Department of State from 1989 to 1993. In 2001, following the election of G.W. Bush, Bolton was appointed undersecretary of state for Arms Control and International Security. Incidentally, President Trump appointed him national security adviser in 2018.

He also served on the United States Commission on International Religious Freedom.

Bolton was US ambassador to the United Nations from 2005 to 2006, a recess appointee.

His abrasive manner and way of presenting ideas ruffled feathers from the start ("Top 10"). Upon Bolton's resignation, one ambassador opined, "Instinctively, he's a bully"; he "has succeeded in putting almost everyone's back up, even among America's closest allies." President George W. Bush, always one to heap praise upon his people, characteristically affirmed, "John Bolton had done a fabulous job." A writer for the *Economist* magazine concluded that John Bolton was "the most controversial ambassador ever sent by America to the United Nations" ("His UNdoing").

During his career in government, Bolton enjoyed close ties to Dick Cheney (Unger, *Fall* 204, 206). Cheney supported Bolton's bid to be named ambassador to the UN. Though a protégé of Jim Baker and Senator Jesse Helms in foreign affairs, Bolton was like all neocons: "a unilateralist who believed that the United States should not negotiate with Iran and North Korea. He did his best to stymie any negotiations during his tenure at the State Department." Notably, he "functioned as a bridge between the neocons and the traditional conservatives" (Heilbrunn 266).

John Bolton was a passionate hawk and friend of Israel. Ever outspoken and often brusque and curt, he was a fierce and confrontational figure. Diligently involved in the vital and polemical work of think tanks, he was associated with the American Enterprise Institute (AEI), Jewish Institute for National Security Affairs, Gatestone Institute, and the Institute of East-West Dynamics, among others.

I. Lewis "Scooter" Libby was born in 1950 in New Haven, Connecticut. In 1972, he earned a BA at Yale University and in 1975 a JD at Columbia Law School. Over the years, Libby alternated practicing law with political activity.

At Yale, Libby singled out Paul Wolfowitz as one of his favorite professors. They became close friends and political colleagues; Wolfowitz tapped him for duty several times in their professional lives. In 1981, after working as a lawyer in the Schnader firm in Philadelphia, Libby accepted Wolfowitz's offer to be a staff member on the State Department's policy planning staff. From 1982 to 1985, Libby directed special projects in the East Asian and Pacific Affairs bureau. Then he went back to practicing law until 1989, when Wolfowitz brought him to the Department of Defense as a deputy undersecretary for strategy and resources.

From 2001 to 2005, Libby held the offices of assistant to the vice president for National Security Affairs, chief of staff to the vice president, and assistant to the president of the United States. Consequently, he was extraordinarily well situated—at the decision-making center of the United States government—to contribute to the adoption of policy directives and other vital areas of national concern. "As chief aide to Vice President Dick Cheney, Libby had been involved in almost every major decision made by the Bush administration" ("Profile"). During this same period, specifically from 2001 to 2003, Libby also worked for the mighty Defense Policy Board when it was chaired by Richard Perle.

In 1992, with fellow neoconservative **Zalmay Khalilzad** (born in Afghanistan, 1951; PhD, University of Chicago), Scooter Libby wrote the highly important Defense Planning Guidance document, a far-reaching recipe on future US defense policy. Later in this report I will discuss the principal function of Libby in shaping this consequential document. Suffice it to say for now, Scooter Libby was a persistent hawk. He did his part energetically, but rather quietly, toward the goal of putting American troops into Iraq.

Scooter Libby, unlike most fellow neocons, did not work in the limelight but was highly effective in the George W. Bush administration. Nonetheless, to appreciate Libby's manner and approach to a task, all one has to do is bring to mind the loquacious presence of Richard Perle and list some of his common behavioral qualities; the opposite qualities were Libby's. As John Dickerson noted, Libby stayed out of the public eye, working on "policy in the shadows" and almost never making a public speech. He was "discreet, big-thinking, detail-oriented, and addicted to action over show." In the critical years, he was in the middle of interactions of the government of the United States. He was there, listening, compiling data to use against Saddam, and offering arguments with measured force and "lack of emotion" (Dickerson). This is not to say, certainly, that Scooter Libby hid his views. He was productive, executing the will of Vice President Cheney and the president at every turn.

Scooter Libby took part in the diplomatic processes involving the United States and other nations. On one interaction related to securing peace between the Israelis and the Palestinians involving Libby and Jack Straw, the Israeli-friendly British foreign secretary Straw had occasion to comment on the behavior of coparticipant Libby, "It's a toss-up whether he is working for the Israelis or the Americans on any given day" (Vogler). Libby's interest in the security of Israel led to a kind of myopia that wiped out the national boundary in his vision; he saw the needs of the US and Israel as unitary, an observation applying to other neoconservative figures.

Libby received many awards for government service: the Foreign Affairs Award for Public Service, United States Department of State, 1985; the Distinguished Service Award, United States Department of Defense, 1993; and the Distinguished Public Service Award, United States Department of the Navy, 1993.

And then in 2002, the US picked up a report from Rome that Saddam of Iraq was planning to create a big bomb and therefore had arranged to secure needed uranium yellowcake from Niger in Africa. CIA Director George Tenet did not quash the story, and it slipped out to the media. The false and frightening message was disseminated in a variety of wordings, but the gist was that proof exists that Saddam Hussein has purchased—or is in the process of purchasing from Niger—the stuff of weapons of mass destruction!

On February 26, 2003, American diplomat Joseph Wilson arranged with the CIA to go to Niger to investigate the claim. In his reportedly thorough inquiry, he found no evidence to corroborate the yellowcake account. On July 6, 2003, Wilson wrote an op-ed piece for the *New York Times* accusing the US administration of having concocted the Niger story as a scare tactic to fan the flames for striking Iraq. Then on July 14, *Washington Post's* conservative columnist Robert Novak surprised his readers by unveiling a secret: Wilson's wife, Valerie Plame, was employed by the CIA as an operative working undercover. Thus, Novak blew her cover, ending her career as a CIA agent.

Later, Novak regretted his expose relating to Plame's employment, saying that he should have ignored it. But in a subsequent interview, he took a different tack—while providing an answer to the "why I did it" question. Yes, he would do it again.

I'd go full speed ahead because of the hateful and beastly way in which my left-wing critics in the press and Congress tried to make a political affair out of it and tried to ruin me. My response now is this: The hell with you. They didn't ruin me. I have my faith, my family, and a good life. A lot of people love me—or like me. So they failed. I would do the same thing over again because I don't think I hurt Valerie Plame whatsoever. (Armbruster)

So, Robert Novak, wounded—and motivated accordingly—defended himself in his fashion.

The National Intelligence Council found to be baseless the story of Saddam Hussein buying or attempting to buy yellowcake, just as Wilson had reported. The nationalist hawk Dick Cheney, though knowing the truth, continued to repeat the lie. The president in his 2003 State of the Union Address, while knowledgeable of the facts, uttered this erroneous sentence: "The British government has learned that Saddam Hussein recently sought significant quantities of uranium from Africa." Those words became known as Bush's "sixteen words of deceit."

Back to Scooter—a national scandal was in the making. In December of 2003, a zealous special prosecutor was appointed to determine if any federal criminal statutes had been violated in the leak about Valerie Plame's CIA employment—and if so, by whom, originally. The prosecutor interviewed dozens of people while the media reported the event. Dick Cheney's chief of staff Scooter Libby testified in 2004, and as it turned out, he was the only White House official found to be implicated in the case, specifically in the leak of Valerie Plame's secret identity.

Libby was indicted on five counts and convicted on four: one on obstruction of justice, two on perjury, and one on making false statements. He was acquitted on one other false statement charge.

Bush commuted his thirty-month prison sentence but did not grant a pardon on the other counts. Later, in an interview on Fox News, when he was asked if he were still hopeful of a pardon, Libby answered despairingly, "I worked 13 years—maybe 12 years—on federal government national security." In the interview, we hear the woe in his voice, the defeat, as he went on in self-defense, citing instances of personal experience that he wanted listeners to appreciate.

> I met Chuck who had his [life spent] under communism; Kurds who suffered under atrocities of Saddam Hussein; and the American families who lost their kids overseas. And in that time, I learned two things. The world is not just. And it doesn't do a lot of good to whine. (Fox News, "Scooter Libby Speaks," *YouTube*)

In review, it becomes apparent that Libby did not answer the exact question posed, i.e., the question of hope on securing a full pardon. A careful examination of the interaction shows that Libby wanted to protect himself through a recounting of his professional life—his long dedication to good works and how he felt about Iraq, still unsecured. His statement can be interpreted thusly: "During all those years, I toiled to defeat the ravages of communism and save people who were being victimized by Saddam and to spare American families from losing their kids overseas." Libby responded to personal urgencies to tell his story: *I have no regrets for what I aimed to do. And, yes, I failed to do it.*

So speaks a man wanting to move on, without *guilt* from wrongdoing but with *shame* for failing in accomplishing his main goal.

David Wurmser was born in Switzerland and has dual citizenship with that country; he has BA, MA, and PhD degrees, all from Johns Hopkins University.

Wurmser served as advisor on the Middle East from 1989 to 1993 to Vice President Dan Quayle and to Arms Control Undersecretary John Bolton from 2001 to 2003.

He held memberships in several think tanks: AEI, Institute for Advanced Strategic and Political Studies (IASPS of Jerusalem), Middle East Forum (MEF), United States Committee for a Free Lebanon, United States Institute of Peace, Washington Institute for Near East Policy (WINEP), and Policy Terrorism Group.

With IASPS in 1996 he was part of a group, led by Richard Perle, that produced *A Clean Break: A New Strategy for Securing the Realm*, a report prepared for Israel's new Prime Minister Benjamin Netanyahu. It urged that Israel take steps to remove Saddam Hussein from his position in Iraq. Other contributors to the message of advice for Israel were Douglas

Feith and Meyrav Wurmser, an active neoconservative, wife of and frequent coauthor with David Wurmser.

David Wurmser was the industrious director of the Middle East program at AEI. And then he became associated with Ahmed Chalabi's Iraqi National Congress, or INC, founded in 1992, a well-organized political insurgency that planned to bring down Saddam Hussein. Wurmser's book of 1999, *Tyranny's Ally: America's Failure to Defeat Saddam Hussein*, displays his belief in the INC cause. *Tyranny's Ally* is an attractively produced book of 160 pages in which Wurmser lays out an array of US mistakes in historic dealings with Iraq and his view of the threat posed by totalitarian states of the Middle East. Throughout the book, the author introduces contentions but without adequate explanation and/or evidence.

With the style chosen, he reveals a view of his intended audience as friendly, and sympathetic to his arguments. He freely and without comment conflates the needs of Israel and the US. And without any clarification, he refers to Israel's "Grapes of Wrath operation" in Lebanon. Though Wurmser's book was written before the political appearance of son George W. Bush, a complete identification of the father in the index and elsewhere would avoid moments of distraction: i.e., for rewards of clarity, Wurmser should give the full "G.H.W." not the bare "George."

A reviewer might continue raising editorial questions, but suffice it to acknowledge that the book was published under the aegis of the AEI. The readers, the probable audience, doubtless applauded in appreciation of the contents. And if the criterion of success in book writing is defined as a function of audience response, Dr. Wurmser very likely succeeded in connecting.

Wurmser was perplexed, lamenting the United States' "defeat of itself by proffering victories to both pan-Arabic nationalism and fundamentalism and by embracing movements that advocate the ideas we discredited in the Cold War."

Though not a summary, this statement on page 136 of the book expresses his thesis.

> Any effort to deal with Iraq and the anti-Americanism in the region must begin with a determination to defeat the destructive policies of pan-Arabism in

Iraq. An effective strategy...must reject all forms of pan-Arabic nationalism as legitimate or productive forces in Arab politics. (Wurmser)

Thus, we understand the burden of David Wurmser, who in his style produced a steady flow of material to advance the cause of regime change in Iraq.

Incidentally, Richard Perle wrote the foreword to Wurmser's book, spending most of his 1,600 words in offering historical data related to America's policy in the Middle East. He describes Wurmser's work as a "study of how the United States must deal with the sort of tyranny that consumed all of our attention during the Cold War and continues to thrive in other parts of the world." Perle urges policymakers to use the book as a guide "in dealing not only with Iraq but with the Middle East as a whole."

Robert James Woolsey, Jr. ("James" or "Jim" or "R. James") was born in 1941. He has a BA from Stanford University, an MA from St. John's College, and an LLB from Yale University. Woolsey was/is a Presbyterian.

Woolsey is a Democrat who served actively under six presidents: Nixon, Carter, Reagan, G.H.W. Bush, Clinton, and G.W. Bush. Perhaps we can count seven presidents, given his service on President Donald Trump's transition team. He resigned in January 2017, taken aback by reports that Trump had plans to make unwelcome changes in the US intelligence structure.

He was involved deeply in arms reduction diplomacy and negotiations with the Soviet Union during the '70s and '80s. From 1969 to 1970 he advised on strategic arms limitation; from 1970 to 1973 he was general counsel to the US Senate Committee on Armed Services; Woolsey served as undersecretary of the Navy from 1977 to 1979 and was the delegate at large to the Strategic Arms Reduction Talks and Nuclear and Space Arms Talks from 1983 to 1986; President G.H.W. Bush appointed him ambassador to the Negotiation on Conventional Armed Forces, where he served from 1989 to 1991; he was director of the CIA from 1993 to 1995 ("Woolsey, James").

As a lawyer, Woolsey was associated over many years with the firm of Shea and Gardner in Washington, DC.

Among his many important memberships
are these: Jewish Institute for National Security
Affairs; Defense Policy Board from 2001 to 2005
(of which colleague Richard Perle was forced to
resign his chairmanship); the Project for the New
American Century; Center for Strategic and
International Studies; Washington Institute for
Near East Policy; Committee on the Present
Danger; and Center for Security Policy.
Woolsey's position on JINSA's Board of Advisers
testifies to his unwavering interest in supporting
causes of Israel and his unstinting advocacy of
an invasion of Iraq (Vest). His leadership in the
hard-line think tank, Foundation for Defense of
Democracies, is also indicative of Woolsey's firm
support of Israel and aggressive approach to
defense of that country. The Foundation was
founded to "build Israel's reputation" in the
United States.

Woolsey, a Democrat, favored Eugene
McCarthy for president in 1968 and opposed the
Vietnam War. He was a hawk on foreign policy
but, like Scoop Jackson, supported social
issues. After 9/11, he was one of the first to aver
that Iraq was involved in the attack, declaiming
that any response would have to include
deposing Saddam Hussein (Fallows).

In the critical fall of 2002, Woolsey fell in line and did much public speaking in promotion of war—delivering the same speech several times—to audiences of numerous venues, e.g., the National War College at National Defense University and a number of military installations. He named a prospective war against Iraq "World War IV," (the one to follow "III," the period of promoting an invasion that started on the heels 9/11). His long address differed markedly from any neoconservative example unearthed in this study. It was not the likes of any rhetorical composition by a Robert Kagan, Ledeen, Wurmser, Wolfowitz, or Perle, etc.

James Woolsey developed many of his arguments in "World War IV" from events in history. It is polemical, yes, but more professorial than a talk made for the hustings, more like a lecture. Though very long, the composition was meant for oral communication and is marked by that conception, to be heard by listeners. In any reception, read or heard, it is less antagonistic, warmer, more reassuring than a statement of Charles Krauthammer. Though lacking in word economy, it has broader appeal than the philosophy of David Brooks. Woolsey's witty mien was attractive to audiences.

The discourse is laden with anecdotes, illusions, cultural observations, comparisons and contrasts, etc. The author called up Albert Einstein, Kofi Anan, Winston Churchill, Earl Warren, and other of his contemporaries, even citing TSA airport workers. Included are references to modern American technology, Belarus, Anglo Saxon origins, and the United States Constitution.

> Terrorists and pathological predators have to realize that now for the fourth time in 100 years, we've been awakened and this country is on the march. We didn't choose this fight, but we're in it. And...there's only one way we're going to be able to win it. It's the way of World War I fighting for Wilson's 14 points. The way we won World War II fighting for Churchill's and Roosevelt's Atlantic Charter and the way we won World War III fighting for the noble ideas I think best expressed by President Reagan, but also very importantly at the beginning by President Truman.

Woolsey advised that his conflict not be construed as typical classical warfare, not as one state opposing a second state.

We have to convince the people of the Middle East that we are on their side, as we convinced Lech Walesa and Vaclav Havel and Andrei Sakharov that we were on their side. This will take time. It will be difficult. But I think we need to say to both the terrorists and the dictators and also to the autocrats who from time to time are friendly with us, that we know, we understand we are going to make you nervous. We want you to be nervous. We want you to realize now for the fourth time in 100 years, this country is on the march and we are on the side of those whom you most fear—your own people. (Woolsey, "World War IV")

Woolsey's rhetorical posture contrasts with the usual neoconservative posture. He is less straightforward, often folksy, frequently acting more as sage than fighter.

Though named a neoconservative, Woolsey regarded the term "silly." Here at the end of his profile, the question must be asked: Does James Woolsey really qualify as a neocon? Or, how do we account for the heavy "pastel" in his rhetorical coloration?

Let's interrupt briefly this profile of James Woolsey and call on Jim Lobe to offer an apt formulation on neocon attributes. His article "Neoconservatism in a Nutshell" is a brilliant distillation of neoconservative beliefs, drawn from many years of observation and study.

The essential elements of the neocons' past fifty years, according to Lobe, are:

- *a Manichean view of a world in which good and evil are constantly at war and the United States has an obligation to lead forces for good around the globe;*

- *a belief in the moral exceptionalism of both the United States and Israel and the absolute moral necessity for the US to defend Israel's security;*

- *a conviction that, in order to keep evil at bay, the United States must have—and be willing to exercise—the military power necessary to defeat any and all challengers (and its corollary: force is the only language that evil understands);*

- *a belief that the 1930s—with Munich, appeasement, Chamberlain, Churchill—*

*taught us everything we need to know
about evil and how to fight it; and*

- *democracy is generally desirable, but it
always depends on who wins.* (Lobe,
"Neoconservatism in a Nutshell")

Contrary to Lobe's criteria, Woolsey does
not describe enemies in terms of black and
white. In the aforementioned "World War IV"
speech (or lecture), he finds three enemies in the
Middle East: (1) the fascists, e.g., Syria, Iraq
(and Libya); (2) totalitarian movements—to wit,
Tehran (the mullahs of Iran); and (3) "the Sunni
side"—the Wahhabi religious conservatives of
Saudi Arabia. Woolsey did not meet the
Manichean specification. Nor does he profess a
view of moral exceptionalism among the peoples
of the US and Israel. Nor in his discourses does
he point to critical failures in Europe in the
1930s.

Moreover, does not Woolsey's abiding
interest in arms reduction during the Cold War
add a datum to the argument against his
membership in the neoconservative corps?

Respected commentators are disposed to
lump Woolsey with the others—the Wurmsers,

Abrams, R. Kagan, and the rest. However, my analysis, using Jim Lobe's criteria, leads to recommending removal of Woolsey from neocon membership.

As we move along in these pages, Jim Lobe's perceptive characterizations will become more meaningful. We might add to his list a criterion relating to strategy: *success of neoconservative persuasiveness is traceable to accomplishment of rhetorical cohesiveness.* Chapter 10 will review that topic.

A Summing Up

Neocons worked tirelessly in think tanks, in various government positions as advisors and consultants, as staff members to elected officials, writers, editors, and speakers, in and out of media outlets, and so forth. The following were among other active and prominent people in the time period of this report: Gary Schmitt; David S. Addington; Stephen Bryen; Danielle Pletka; Max Boot; Joshua Muravchik; Bernard Lewis; Donald Kagan—father to neocon Frederick Kagan (and Robert)—David Frum; Michael Rubin; Kenneth Adelman; Eliot Cohen; Paula Dobriansky; Robert B. Zoellick; Frank Gaffney; Peter W. Rodman; Reuel Marc Gerecht;

Aaron Friedberg; Eric Breindel; Dov Zakheim; and Midge Decter. Of course, scores of other men and women, though not listed here—lesser lights—are nonetheless diligent contributors to all circuits of information dedicated to furthering the persuasion.

As often observed, most neoconservatives were Jewish, and they stood together in promoting an invasion of Iraq. But where did American Jews in general stand? An exploration in the *New York Times* of March 15, 2003, provides useful information (Goodstein, "Threats"). All following citations on the subject are from Laurie Goodstein's piece.

> Most Christian denominations have taken a stand against going to war. But while individual Jews have been prominent in antiwar events and proclamations, Jewish groups have said little that is either explicitly opposed to, or in favor of, a war.

In early March of 2003, Hannah Rosenthal, executive director of the Jewish Council for Public Affairs, reported "no consensus" among 700 leaders of all four Jewish branches. Rabbi Eric Yoffie, president of the Union of American Hebrew Congregations, found "profound ambivalence." Other leaders found "no consensus" or members' being as "divided as the rest of the nation" or unlikely to "reach agreement."

David A. Harris, executive director of the American Jewish Committee, offers an accurate statement: a number of Jews working in the administration's foreign policy team have long advanced the strategy of a preemptive war against Mr. Hussein.

Finally, in the last citation from the *New York Times* article are data on polling which may add to our understanding.

> Several polls have found that Jews are less likely than the public at large to support military action against Iraq. An aggregate of surveys conducted by the Pew Research Center from August 2002 to February 2003 found 52 percent of Jews in favor of military action, 32 percent opposed and 16 percent uncertain; among all Americans, the polling found 62 percent in favor, 28 percent opposed and 10 percent uncertain.

3

Think Tanks

Functions of Think Tanks

In a rhetorical sense, a think tank is inventional, i.e., it is an operation that facilitates discovery of material for practical use in the creation of persuasive messages. It is a facility for—a means to—developing briefs which rhetors consult, alone or in organizations of influence. As provider of choices, the think tank is invaluable.

Most neoconservatives took full advantage of think tanks built to accommodate their promotional interests, particularly in locating the stuff of messages and building briefs. Advocates put these organizations to good use and relied heavily on them.

The business of a think tank is advocacy, influence, persuasion. Members of think tanks conduct research, and they write and speak, argue and refute, listen and collaborate. They weigh strategies for getting out the established word in an effective way to a responsive audience in vast arrays of settings: key organizations and key people—and at the best time. With their newsletters, books, articles, studies, and face-to face opportunities, they are employed to reach people and organizations, to impact policy (Fawal).

Members, often called "fellows," commonly have a staff to help with processing information, assisting in research on papers and reports, and locating fit audiences. Staff workers engage the press and people who run websites, manage events, and compose newsletters and other types of communicative structures—all of whose jobs deal with finding available channels to process important messages for domestic or world distribution. Most countries have think tanks (McGann).

The **Middle East Forum**, with roots back to 1990, remains active today. Its members—especially Daniel Pipes—work diligently, looking after the US-Israeli relationship, arguing the advantages of that connection, and acting energetically in promotion of its palpable end.

Daniel Pipes was born in 1949 in Boston. He graduated from Harvard University in 1971 with an AB and in 1978 with a PhD, both in history.

Pipes is a scholar with a rich background in Islamic studies. He is a historian of the Islamic Middle East who spent three years in Egypt and learned to read Arabic. He studied Muslim philosophers and the Quran.

In his career, Pipes held few government positions. He was appointed to the Department of Defense's special task force on terrorism in November 2001 and was a board member of the US Institute of Peace, 2003 to 2005.

Most of the following three paragraphs of data are from Pipes' "Biography of Daniel Pipes."

In his busy career, he lectured at the Naval War College, Harvard University, University of Chicago, and the University of Pennsylvania. He has appeared on many television programs, e.g., *Crossfire, Good Morning America, The News-Hour with Jim Lehrer, Nightline, The O'Reilly Factor,* and foreign television networks, such as BBC and Al-Jazeera.

The Middle East Forum is a relatively small think tank but is ambitious and makes a huge presence. The indefatigable Daniel Pipes, founder and principal spokesperson, stated the MEF's scope in oblique terms: "The Middle East Forum promotes American interests in the Middle East and protects the Constitutional order from Middle Eastern threats" (Pipes, "Middle East Forum").

Daniel Pipes, was/is the out-front spokesperson for the MEF, committed to declaiming the threat posed by "Islamists" to the welfare of Israel and the United States, the two nations taken together.

Beginning in 2002, Pipes led an MEF activity called "Campus Watch," which monitored US educational programs on Middle East studies, gathering information on offerings and investigating content and its handling. It reported on erring institutions and professors' activities, inviting "student complaints of abuse." ("Campaign Launched").

No neoconservative figure labored more tirelessly than Daniel Pipes. In Chapter 6, we shall expand on his extraordinary contributions as a writer.

The **Washington Institute for Near East Policy**, an expansive think tank, was established in 1985. The stated mission was "to advance a balanced and realistic understanding of American interests in the Middle East and to promote the policies that secure them" ("Mission & History"). The founding director, Martin Indyk, shaped WINEP into an aggressive think tank that sought to strengthen the relationship of US to Israel's conservative ruling party ("Peace"). Formerly, Indyk had been the research director of the American Israel Public Affairs Committee, AIPAC, the most powerful pro-Israel lobby in the US.

Members of WINEP included familiar neocons: Robert Kagan, Joshua Muravchik, Daniel Pipes, and James Woolsey, as well as prominent politicians: Madeleine K. Albright, Sandy Berger, Howard Berman, and Dennis Ross.

WINEP's directors and board members, all formidable advocates, appeared often on talk shows and disseminated their messages with impressive success, e.g., in periodicals and books, on websites and broadcast outlets, and through reporters and leaders in many fields. Their creation of a great variety of strategies to reach people and organizations is exemplary ("Mission & History").

Every four years they convened a
"bipartisan blue-ribbon commission" known as
the Presidential Study Group, which presented a
guidance proposal to the newly elected United
States president a well-prepared "blueprint for
Middle East policy" (Whitaker, "US Thinktanks").

The **American Enterprise Institute** is a
mammoth think tank with multiple
involvements and branch activities dealing with
conservative issues and advocacy: employing
intellectuals and other professionals to study
and prepare right-wing material to be used by
influential persons and organizations. It
cooperated with like-minded entities in
furtherance of free-market policy, individual
opportunity, and military preparedness. Since
the '80s, it has encouraged into membership
prominent neoconservatives.

On the evening of February 26, 2003,
President Bush gave a brief address at a meeting
of the American Enterprise Institute, convened
at the Washington Hilton Hotel. In his
introduction he singled out notable members in
attendance, e.g., Justices Scalia and Thomas—
and Vice President Cheney ["Thank God Dick
Cheney said 'yes' when, in 1999, we asked him
to be on our election ticket as running mate,"

said Mr. Bush]. Bush referred to about twenty
AEI members "on loan," borrowed from his
administration, "some of the finest minds in our
nation....I want to thank them for their service."
He was referring to neocons hired by his
administration, many of whom have been
discussed or mentioned in these pages: AEI
members John Bolton, Richard Perle, Paul
Wolfowitz, Frederick Kagan, Michael Ledeen,
David Frum, Douglas Feith, and David
Wurmser.

The president went on in his speech,
stressing the lesson learned on September 11,
2001, and relied on a falsehood: "In Iraq, a
dictator is building and hiding weapons that
could enable him to dominate the Middle East
and intimidate the civilized world—and we will
not allow it."

He affirmed that when the threat of terror
is removed, peace will come, and then "the new
government of Israel...will be expected to
support the creation of a viable Palestinian
state" [applause]; then "settlement activities in
the occupied territories must end" [applause]
(Office of the Press Secretary, "President
Discusses").

As we now know, the new Israeli government, led by Likud's Benjamin Netanyahu, would not fulfill those two expectations of President Bush.

That evening, February 26, 2003, the president held back in announcing a big event: that in three weeks the membership of the American Enterprise Institute would be seeing an Iraqi fireworks display on their TVs. "Shock and Awe," a display of military might as it was designated, would be seen lighting the Baghdad skyline.

The **Jewish Institute for National Security Affairs** was powerful. Though Israel was the victor in the war with Arab states in 1973, that event awakened the nation to an urgent need to build a stronger defense structure. Thus, it turned to the United States and to the formation of a think tank, JINSA, "to educate the American public of the importance of an effective US defense capability so that our vital interests as Americans can be safeguarded." The goal as stated made a clear assumption of a mutual security connection of the two nations, a frequent claim appearing in neocon literature.

JINSA was formed in 1977, with Michael Ledeen as executive director. He was followed by Stephen Bryen in 1979, whose leadership brought the group into full functioning as an effective undertaking.

Especially interesting and unique among structures of think tanks is JINSA's annual military visit. Each year since the 1980s, the organization has sponsored a program involving retired United States flag military officers visiting Israel for a period—ten days or so—to meet with their counterparts in the Israeli military. They visit Israeli army and navy bases and other installations and become acquainted with personnel and operations, effecting a tightening of the ties between the countries at the armed-forces leadership level. Writer Jason Vest commented sardonically, suggesting the JINSA expectation: when the US officers get back home, they "happily write op-eds and sign letters and advertisements championing the Likudnik [Israeli conservative] line" (Vest).

JINSA also conducts a visitation event for selected cadets from US military academies to learn about security issues with Israelis (Milstein).

Early active JINSA supporters or board members included neocons Stephen Bryen, John Bolton, Elliott Abrams, Douglas Feith, Jeane Kirkpatrick, Richard Perle, Joshua Muravchik, and James Woolsey. Also serving were Senator Joseph Lieberman, Richard Cheney, and Congressman Jack Kemp.

JINSA faithfully honored Senator Henry M. Jackson:

> Each year since 1982, the Jewish Institute for National Security Affairs awards a Henry M. "Scoop" Jackson Distinguished Service Award to a person for his or her career-long dedication to the security of the United States. The first recipient of the award, before it was named in his honor after his death in 1983, was Senator Jackson, in 1982. (Cornfield)

The **Hudson Institute** is a large study and promotional organization—think tank—that was founded in 1961 by a group of intellectuals that included futurist Herman Kahn. Among their several major achievements was the creation of formulations on nuclear deterrence strategy. Hudson became famous for its predictions of future events and has mounted the Initiative on Future Innovation.

Among other notable Hudson figures are Alexander Haig, Donald Kagan, Henry Kissinger, Robert Bork, Abram Shulsky, Dan Quayle, and Mitch Daniels—all familiar political figures.

As the Institute developed, it structured much of its work as centers, e.g., Center for Religious Freedom, Center for Global Prosperity, and Center for Middle Eastern Policy. Titles change as interests in issues change. Over time, members have been committed to the investigation of trends in the ideology of Islam. After 9/11, Hudson spent much energy on Iraq. One of their busiest sections has been the Center on Islam, Democracy, and the Future of the Muslim World.

With this introduction to the Hudson Institute, we will go to a profile of one notable member: Meyrav Wurmser directed the Center for Middle East Policy. **Meyrav Wurmser** is an American, born in Israel. She earned a PhD degree in political science at George Washington University in 1998.

She taught at Johns Hopkins University and the US Naval Academy.

She is married to David Wurmser, an active neoconservative profiled above.

She was a Senior Fellow at the Hudson Institute and a member of the **Endowment for Middle East Truth** (EMET, meaning "truth" in Hebrew). She was a contributing expert to the **Ariel Center for Policy Research** and held membership in **the Institute for Advanced Strategic and Political Studies.**

In 1996, as mentioned above, she participated with Richard Perle, David Wurmser, and Douglas Feith in preparing *A Clean Break: A New Strategy for Securing the Realm*, a paper of advisement for incoming Israeli Likud (Conservative Party) prime minister, Benjamin Netanyahu.

Meyrav Wurmser was a cofounder in 1998 and executive director of the **Middle East Media Research Institute**, or MEMRI. Donald Rumsfeld, John Bolton, Bernard Lewis, Norman Podhoretz, Daniel Pipes, and James Woolsey have been members of the advisory board. MEMRI dealt with Muslim topics, specializing in translating publications written in various Middle Eastern languages. The purpose of the institute was to disseminate English translations of Middle Eastern media in order to close the language gap, making information available on Arab cultures. To wit—MEMRI sought to reveal anti-Semitic or anti-American rhetoric disseminated in the Middle East. It backed the Israeli government and American neoconservatives in their campaign to put the best light on the West and Israel. Meyrav Wurmser's group was selective in reporting on Middle Eastern writings, particularly of the press. "To anyone who reads Arabic newspapers regularly, it should be obvious that the items highlighted by Memri are those that suit its agenda and are not representative of the newspapers' content as a whole" (Rosenau). Strategic translation is MEMRI's niche.

In 2002, Brian Whitaker of *The Guardian* newspaper wrote a piece on his frequent receipt of free MEMRI translations of articles in Arabic newspapers. Of high quality, the "emails also go to politicians and academics, as well as to lots of other journalists" (Whitaker, "Selective").

Wurmser's MEMRI was accused of providing "misleading translations that heighten the impression of anti-Semitic or anti-American rhetoric in the Middle East"; the translations have been labeled as "Islamophobia" (Marusek

and Miller). In 2005, with the Iraq invasion
under way, MEMRI supported a film project
dealing with defamatory material. In the fall of
2005, Clarion, an organization with the goal of
"challenging radical Islam," made a very
expensive film called *Obsession: Radical Islam's
War Against the West.* The ostensible aim of the
film was to influence the election of John
McCain. It was anti-Muslim in content, depicting
Islam as a despicable and deadly threat to the
West in general and to the US and Israel in
particular. It was over sixty minutes in length
and distributed as a DVD. Meyrav Wurmser's
EMET assisted with distribution. Twenty-eight
million copies of the film were enclosed as an
advertising supplement in seventy-four
newspapers, including the *New York Times* and
the *Chronicle of Higher Education* (Shatz, "Short
Cuts"). Five newspapers refused to distribute the
DVD.

The drama depicted in the *Obsession* film
is inflammatory, carried by the expert narration
of talented men and women, some of whom bear
Arabic names. Well-known American figures
have important parts in the documentary, e.g.,
neoconservative Daniel Pipes, one of those
profiled above. The accompanying intense music
and penetrating sound effects were carefully

chosen to enhance the message, as were all the high-quality cinematic devices (Clarion Project; "Obsession—Radical Islam," *YouTube*).

The lengthy segment on comparing Hitler's Nazism to current Islamic philosophy and behavior is hateful in goal and content. Bothersome questions of morality and propriety arise as one views this production. In construction, the documentary is a first-class work of propaganda. Morally, it is highly objectionable.

When a Muslim advocacy group in 2008 filed a complaint about the film, EMET withdrew support (Fingerhut). But Meyrav Wurmser's mission to teach about the political threat of Islam continued.

Among other notable US think tanks are the Brookings Institution, the Heritage Foundation, Carnegie Endowment for International Peace, Claremont Institute, and Lexington Institute.

4

Chalabi

Ahmed [Ahmad] Chalabi, 1944–2015

Ahmed Chalabi, the scion of a wealthy Iraqi family, fled the country as the 1958 Baath revolution began. He spent most of the rest of his life in other parts of the Middle East, Britain, and the United States, always with the hope of returning to Iraq as leader of the country. Consequently, he chose active roles in the lead-up to the 2003 invasion of Iraq. With contacts in his home country, he was often a helpful resource.

Chalabi attended universities in the United States and graduated from MIT with an MA. He studied under Albert Wohlstetter at the University of Chicago, earning a PhD degree in 1969. Thus, he made an early connection to neoconservative activity.

Early on, in other countries of the Middle East, he built a fortune in business enterprises, and when accused of illegal banking practices in

Jordan in 1989, he fled to London. Ultimately, he built connections in the US, where he became involved in the Iraqi National Congress, a political organization supported by Americans working toward regime change in Iraq. He believed that participation in the INC would lead to control in Iraq when regime change was accomplished there (see Chan; Isikoff and Corn 49–53; Mayer; and Dizard).

Chalabi became acquainted with American neoconservatives, who welcomed him to join their march toward the takeover of Iraq. He created ties with influential persons at the Pentagon, e.g., Deputy Secretary of Defense Paul Wolfowitz, Under Secretary of Defense Douglas Feith, and Deputy Under Secretary of Defense William J. Luti. Wolfowitz, in particular, was taken with Chalabi, a friend of Chalabi reported that "Chalabi really charmed him" (Mayer). Importantly, Chalabi created a friendship with Vice President Dick Cheney.

Chalabi, in his association with US neoconservatives, envisioned conquering Iraq "as the precondition for a reorganization of the Middle East that would solve Israel's strategic problems." He gave assurance to neocons that Iraq would adopt a receptive and favorable

government. Rest assured, he promised, the new
Iraqi democracy will join with Israel, dismissing
Arab nationalism. He would set up profitable
trade deals for Israel, with their companies
invited to do business in Iraq. He "would agree
to rebuild the pipeline from Mosul (in the
northern Iraqi oil fields) to Haifa," the Israeli
port, and there he would locate a major refinery.
The smooth talker made additional promises of
benefits to accrue to Israel, and he was heeded—
for a time. Chalabi

> appears to have recognized that the
> neocons, while ruthless, realistic and
> effective in bureaucratic politics, were
> remarkably ignorant about the situation in
> Iraq, and willing to buy a fantasy of how
> the country's politics worked. So he sold it
> to them. (Dizard)

Relatedly, "being sold" is an apt phrase to
label a number of topics in this study. For
instance, in investigating the setup of the US
invasion, one occasionally comes across
statements indicating neoconservative ignorance
or misinterpretation of Iraqi cultural
phenomena. "They wanted it so much, they fell
for it" is a suitable paraphrasing. In their fervent
hope, they "were sold" (see Dizard).

Chalabi expressed certainty that Iraq had factories for making WMDs, and he positioned the Iraqi National Congress to facilitate an eventual workable transition to Iraqi democracy. To that end, he specialized in gathering garrulous Iraqi defectors who would fabricate the WMD goings-on in Iraq. One notorious defector was Rafid Ahmed Alwan al-Janabi, or "Curveball," as he was called. His phony reports were used by partisans to demonstrate the need to remove Saddam Hussein. Some of his lies about Iraq's construction of biological-weapon labs were retold by Secretary of State Colin Powell in his speech at the UN on February 5, 2003 (Drogin and Goetz).

The bulk of Chalabi's information on Saddam's WMDs was found to be contrived and false, but not before being widely disseminated. As his data were picked up and spread by the media, the world saw a fanning of the flames by the war hawks.

The *New York Times'* Judith Miller

A striking example of Chalabi's clever work is his
cooperation with journalist Judith Miller. In late
2001 and through 2002, she wrote a long string
of front-page reports for the *New York Times*,
alleging proliferation of WMDs in Iraq (Massing
36–40). One of Judith Miller's manipulations
was her making the "perfect deal" with the White
House. Her modus operandi involved Ahmed
Chalabi providing the Bush White House with
dramatic WMD evidence for their political needs
and his giving the same material to Miller. When
Chalabi gave her something, she went to the
White House and learned that they already
received it from Chalabi. In this way, she had it
corroborated by some White House insider
whom she identified as a "senior administration
official." Thus, she told the world that the US
leadership was aware of Saddam's "evil"
enterprises. She worked the same practical
strategy with the Pentagon (Moore).

Ahmed Chalabi helped make Judith Miller
a journalistic star. The *New York Times* approved
her hokum, and her name was seen on the first
page.

Michael Massing found that the *New York Times* gave more credence to Iraqi defectors' claims on the existence of WMDs than to inspectors' reports on their nonexistence (Massing).

Fourteen months after the invasion, the *New York Times* felt constrained to make an apology, while reporting ignorance of the truth. The newspaper published a euphemistic and superficial confession, patently a flabby, evasive account, in May of 2004.

> We have found...instances of coverage that was not as rigorous as it should have been....In some cases, the information that was controversial then, and seems questionable now, was insufficiently qualified or allowed to stand unchallenged. Looking back, we wish we had been more aggressive in re-examining the claims as new evidence emerged—or failed to emerge....We consider the story of Iraq's weapons, and of the pattern of misinformation, to be unfinished business. And we fully intend to continue aggressive reporting aimed at setting the record straight. (From the Editors)

The *Times* made no follow-up statement on its pro-war stance. No real mea culpa. The prestigious journal continued with daily publication of news, while the ugly war dragged on. Regarding complicity of US newspapers in attacking Iraq, see the findings and observations of Michael Massing (*Now They Tell Us*).

Laurie Mylroie

Extending the Judith Miller story allows us to introduce the bizarre case of Harvard PhD, and later fellow at Harvard University's Center for Middle Eastern Studies, Laurie Mylroie. In 1990, Miller and Mylroie collaborated to produce *Saddam Hussein and the Crisis in the Gulf*, a book devoted to laying bare purported instances of the brutalities committed by Iraqi strong man Saddam Hussein. With sponsorship of the American Enterprise Institute, Mylroie wrote another fanciful book on the threat of terrorism, *Study of Revenge: Saddam Hussein's Unfinished War Against America*. In this work, she found Saddam Hussein to be the perpetrator of the 1993 World Trade Center bombing, the bombing of the federal building in Oklahoma City, and several other disastrous events, including 9/11.

In a word, "Mylroie became enamored of her theory that Saddam was the mastermind of a vast anti-US terrorist conspiracy in the face of virtually all evidence and expert opinion to the contrary" (Bergen, "Did one woman's obsession"). Her incredible arguments alleging involvement of the Iraqi dictator were endorsed and disseminated by like-minded neoconservatives. Among Mylroie's fans were fellow war promoters Richard Perle, Paul Wolfowitz, and James Woolsey. The applause of such known figures influenced acceptance of her baseless views on incidences of Saddam's far-flung and multiple terroristic operations. Hers is a case of success in creation of hysteria leading to convictions based on falsehood.

The story of Ahmed Chalabi's war promotion will be continued in the following chapter.

5

Managing Perceptions

Selling an Invasion

Perhaps this section should not be set off, since all preceding pages are about *selling*—promoting—an invasion of Iraq. It was an early and continued mission of neoconservatives, certainly. Nonetheless, the vital importance of focused expertise at work in choosing an audience and touching up messages justifies singling out specific organizations employed in the process. Thus, the selling job was often mediated by a professional agency, a *public relations* service.

Neoconservative activists created and packaged messages that warned of the threat of Saddam and distributed their exigent material to the full array of mass media outlets. They had at hand a great variety of rhetorical resources. Often, they called upon think tank members, or other long-time associates, or people with other ties, to assist in opening up opportunities to

create news bits, op-ed pieces, talking points—
all the other varieties of strategies and influence.
Most neocon partisans were admirably skilled in
argument and debate. Some had connections to
media leaders, who could arrange for TV talk
and radio shows or opportunities with various
media. Thus, they continued adding to a
national swell of commanding data in their work
of persuasion.

To help in meeting the pressing need,
public relations firms came into prominence and
were available to clients who needed
introduction to promising venues.

Eleana (Eliana) Benador

Almost all Americans owned at least one
television and radio; a high percentage read
magazines and newspapers. Neocons were eager
to fill the maw, as frequently reported (see
Hagan; Lobe, "Andean"; Cohler-Esses,
"Bunkum"). In 2001, Peru-born, Swiss-American
Eleana (also, Eliana) Benador formed "Benador
Associates," an unusual public relations
institution that promised to provide appropriate
outlets for the neoconservative's crafted
material. And more.

Audiences of millions, for instance, saw and heard an interview of Richard Perle on a critical security challenge, found an article by Robert Kagan urging the US to plan for war, and scanned an urgent tract of Max Boot, offered in the op-ed pages. A common and valued assignment for a neocon was a speaking engagement at a big regional or national TV event. Some audiences would be huge, eminent national opinion leaders among them. Thanks to Benador's first-rate speakers' bureau, such a valued placement was available.

Benador had worked with Daniel Pipes at his Middle East Forum starting in 2000, but immediately following 9/11, she started her public relations company, with the backing of Jim Woolsey and A. M. Rosenthal of *New York Times* fame. Clients included many of the most prominent hawks dedicated to strengthening US foreign policy in the Middle East, whose inducements she distributed to the existing media of the day, e.g., the *New York Times*, *Washington Post, Wall Street Journal,* and *Los Angeles Times*. On her roster of clientele were Michael Ledeen, Michael Rubin, Frank Gaffney, Charles Krauthammer, and Max Boot. Benador Associates also touted the talents of Meyrav Wurmser, whom, Eleana advertised, will make a

"radio or television show a unique one"
(Rosenau).

She called her clients "just a bunch of
sensible peace-lovers," often pampering them,
always following through in handling their
productions and taking good care of them and
their ideas. "Benador not only got them the gigs,
she also crafted the theme and made sure they
all stayed on message" (Cockburn and St. Clair,
End Times, 190). Their business was her
business; her clients' arguments were hers.
Colloquially put, "She was family," and "her
heart was in it."

Certain neocons of prominence were not
charged a fee by Eleana Benador, e.g., Jim
Woolsey and Richard Perle. They had supported
her, and consequently, it was an honor to serve
them. For Perle, she provided appearances with
most major TV networks and some
independents. Two days before the invasion, as
it happened, Benador Associates organized a
seminar at Washington's National Press Club to
"support the fight for the people of Iraq." Richard
Perle was the chief participant. Others were
Kanan Makiya, Khidhir Hamza, and other Iraqi
expatriates, all consorts of Ahmed Chalabi and
the Iraqi National Congress (Hagan).

Eleana Benador was a well-backed, focused, and energetic woman of business, with a single goal in "the war of perception management": to flood the nation with attractive reasons for taking up arms (St. Clair, "War Pimps"). Obviously, she loved her work and was admirably suited for it. Her business thrived, and for her part she must be counted a major figure in the great persuasion toward sending troops to Iraq.

John W. Rendon

Actually, the service called *perception management* has been available to governments and businesses for years. The Rendon Group, a vigorous American firm of international scope, was hired to put a good light on numerous US military involvements over the years, e.g., the fighting in Kosovo, the invasion of Panama in 1989, and the war in Afghanistan. By the turn of the century, Rendon had devised much of the war-against-terrorism strategy.

> The firm's head is a rumpled, dough-faced man named John W. Rendon. Since the first Bush administration, he's been on the scene at almost every American military action. During the Panama invasion, he

bunkered in a high-rise on Punta Paitilla with the leaders of the anti-Noriega coalition. In the Gulf War, he set up shop in Taif, Saudi Arabia, to spin on behalf of the exiled Kuwaiti emir. (Foer)

In the new century and the mounting of the case against Iraq, Rendon was hired to tell the world of the threat to peace that was Saddam Hussein's Iraq. Rendon made it into a frightening story of the continuing manufacture of chemical and biological weapons—probably nuclear, all WMDs. Since 9/11, his company has received many millions from the Pentagon for PR services (Bamford, "The Man"; Hedges).

The group also worked with Ahmed Chalabi, the Iraqi figure involved in US foreign affairs. Rendon assisted in creating the Iraqi National Congress and in setting up a plan to install the Iraqi expatriate Chalabi as head of that country when Saddam was deposed.

From the occasional union of Chalabi and Rendon came the strategy of tapping warmongering impulses latent among Americans. A purpose was to teach them to want war. In this, the Rendon Group called up Middle Easterners to testify. In December of 2001, they found a glib man with a dramatic story to tell. Adnan Ihsan Saeed al-Haideri, an Iraqi from Kurdistan, himself committed to removing Saddam from power, claimed to know all about Saddam's WMD program. He said that he had seen the weapons being manufactured in a number of locales in Iraq. Thus, Chalabi and Rendon secured a valuable source of "first-hand information" on Saddam's avid and massive arms development. They accumulated material and then artfully dressed it to manage America's perceptions on conditions in Iraq (Bamford, "The Man").

Al-Haideri enthralled his American handlers with imaginative and convincing tales of Saddam's specific places used to construct WMDs. After the invasion, during the occupation, he was accompanied to the spots in Iraq that he had identified in his warnings. He was unable to show a single site. His allegations on Saddam's manufacturing occupation were completely bogus. Al-Haideri was an accomplished liar, as were the others of Chalabi's and Rendon's recruits from the Middle East who continued to arrive with personal narratives.

We will add a dimension to the significance of the Chalabi-Rendon-neoconservative relationship in promoting the invasion of Iraq when we bring in the Office of Special Plans and discuss further the origin of that phony grist for the neocon mill and how it was skillfully ground.

6

Writers

Three Popular Columnists

A number of neoconservative writers in journalism singled out Iraq and argued for a buildup of US arms. In this regard, columnists Tom Friedman, David Brooks, and Charles Krauthammer were well known. Let's contrast their widely read writings, treating the compositions with application of classical modes of rhetorical appeal: *ethos*, *logos*, and *pathos*.

A *New York Times* columnist, **Tom Friedman**, was born in 1953 in Minneapolis and received a BA from Brandeis University and an MA from Oxford University. He is a clever writer, often laying out his main argument with an appealing metaphor, maybe with some irony sprinkled in, and at times with the ethos of a folksy "now-here's-the-angle-guys" attitude.

Just two weeks before the invasion, Friedman wrote a piece, sensing accurately that war was imminent, only days away.

What you now see unfolding before your eyes is the last few minutes of a game of geopolitical chicken between George Bush and Saddam Hussein....The "funniest line of the week" was Saddam's spokesman's explanation of why Iraqi TV didn't show Saddam destroying missiles, as has been demanded: because if the Iraqi people saw this, they would be so angry at the U.N. there's just no telling what they might do....Right, and if my grandmother had wheels, she'd be a bus.

Saddam is afraid, said Friedman.

The minute he looks less ferocious, he is in danger from those around him....Saddam is finally doing some real disarming, not because the U.N. sent more inspectors...but because Mr. Bush sent the 101st Airborne to Kuwait....brace yourself for the crash and hope for the best—because we're all in the back seat. (Friedman, "Chicken")

A mixing of metaphors is justified if it is rhetorically useful, certainly if the author is popular Tom Friedman.

He won three Pulitzer Prizes.

Weekly Standard author **David Brooks**
was born in Toronto in 1961 and earned a BA at
the University of Chicago. He often chooses to
lay out a philosophical or historical essay. Like
other skilled and patient authors, he shaped his
audience over time. His wide-ranging discourses
were commonly—but not always—logos-
oriented. He expected his readers to follow along
as he brought them to the point of his message.

In a treatment of Michel Aflaq, a
significant figure in Arab history, Brooks
inductively reduces all explored data to the
Baathist identity of Saddam Hussein of Iraq.

> The United States and its democracy must
> be humiliated and brought low so that the
> dominance of the Arab nation can achieve
> its final and fitting triumph, and so realize
> God's plan for the earth....In dealing with
> Saddam...we are not dealing with a
> normal thug or bully, but with a
> missionary whose lofty ideology has not
> changed in four decades....The Baathist
> ideology requires continual conflict and
> bloodshed. Saddam likes to call himself
> The Struggler, and his rule has been
> marked by incessant strife....The Baathist
> ideology allows no remorse over the mass

murder of those who belong to racially
inferior groups....The regime is not just
one evil man; it is a party structure
organized around a transcendent ideology,
an ideology that produced the monster
Saddam, but that is bigger than any
individual. (Brooks, "Saddam's Brain")

Charles Krauthammer was born in 1950
in New York City. He graduated from McGill
University, studied at Balliol College, Oxford,
and was awarded an MD degree from Harvard
University. As writer for the *Washington Post*, he
was frequently pugilistic, fighting angrily against
enemies of ignorance, lethargy, and indifference.
From *pathos*, he argued clamorously for the
invasion of Iraq, exhorting in a fashion that
might be put thusly: "Look, terrorists are killing
us!"; "get off your duffs!"; "right now!" His prize-
winning pieces (he won a Pulitzer) appeared in
hundreds of US newspapers. Incidentally, his
medical speciality at Harvard was psychiatry.
Mr. Krauthammer died in 2018.

His reaction to the attack on the United
States, the column of September 12, 2001, is
largely *pathetic*, as this excerpt will reveal:

This is not crime. This is war....Franklin
Roosevelt did not   respond to Pearl
Harbor by pledging to bring the
commander of Japanese naval aviation to
justice. He pledged to bring Japan to its
knees....You rain destruction on
combatants...fanatical suicide
murderers...who go to their deaths joyfully
deadly....Vicious warriors...willing to kill
thousands of innocents while they kill
themselves are not cowards. They are
deadly, vicious warriors and need to be
treated as such. (Krauthammer)

Taking advantage of 9/11, the ever-ready
and omnipresent neoconservatives pulled out all
stops to awaken the country to the threat of
terrorism. Dramatically framing the struggle as
good versus evil, while largely dismissing al-
Qaeda as the immediate foe, they pointed the
finger at Iraq as the evil one. Or they attempted
to prove that al-Qaeda and Iraq worked together
in creating terror.

Two More Giants

Robert Kagan and William Kristol worked together often, particularly as writers. They were masters of the craft who went to the heights as contributors to neoconservative literature. Kagan's introducing Kristol to the idea of hegemony was the most dramatic event in their productive relationship (Heilbrunn 213–227.) Let's treat them apart, giving each individual attention.

Robert Kagan was born in 1958 in Athens, Greece; he earned a BA at Yale, an MA at Harvard, and in 1980 a PhD in American history at American University.

Kagan was on the State Department planning staff from 1984 to 1988 and, during that period, was a speechwriter for Secretary of State George Shultz. He was a fellow with the Carnegie Endowment for International Peace, senior fellow at the Brookings Institution, and a columnist for the *Washington Post*.

He and William Kristol founded the Project for the New American Century in 1997, one of the first think tanks to stand openly for removing Saddam Hussein and one of the most influential.

Kagan was an intense believer in the importance of the US' maintaining preponderant might in the world; "benevolent hegemony exercised by the United States is good for a vast portion of the world's population" ("Kagan"; R. Kagan, "Benevolent").

His involvement in think tanks was limited, but in other work he was, and is, fruitful. He wrote several books on American foreign policy, e.g., *Dangerous Nation, Twilight Struggle, Of Paradise and Power,* and others more recently. His articles appeared in the *New York Times, New Republic, Weekly Standard,* and *Wall Street Journal,* among other periodicals.

Robert Kagan has made appearances on TV interview shows and networks, like C-SPAN, and *Frontline.* Audio presentations are available for some. Vocally, his principal advantage is his expressiveness: spontaneity and ample variety in style. Obviously, his confidence in purpose led to a freedom in speech delivery, which contributed to his success in communication ("Meet Robert Kagan").

Immediately after 9/11, he and William
Kristol and other neoconservatives sought
vigorously—and wrongly—to remove al-Qaeda
from the American focus, putting the blame for
the attack on Saddam Hussein of Iraq. He
observed that evidence on the involvement of
Iraq in "the horrific attacks of September 11 are
beginning to accumulate: We are at war....The
sacrifices we will make will be fully justified"
(Kagan and Kristol, "Right War"). In this call to
arms, the assertion on accumulation of evidence
is not true but one frequently made after 9/11.

In November of 2002, Kagan joined again
with Kristol, this time writing a long piece for the
Weekly Standard, discussing many conditions
relating to the status of the mission to promote
foreign policy intervention ("The U.N. Trap?"). In
this well-wrought essay, the authors combined
knowledge and power in composition to push for
continuation of the drive to trigger an attack of
Iraq. They began with a salute to President Bush
for his carrying candidates to victory in the off-
year national election and tied it to the
president's war on terrorism.

> If it is true, as we believe, that Bush's
> stature as commander in chief helped put
> Republicans over the top, it is also true

that the president's commitment to Saddam's ouster is part of what has defined his execution of his duties as commander in chief.

These words—this bit of praise directed to the president—is quite significant. Though seemingly a secondary thought, it is meant to reinforce President Bush on his wisdom, to acknowledge his effectiveness and unswerving leadership in the progress toward deposing the dictator. After 9/11, such boosting was a common neocon act of suasion on maintaining the pressure and staying focused. It was part of the "full court press," the intense urging alluded to earlier. In this instance, the message for Bush might be put, *"You're doing fine, Sir; stay with it—and don't let down."*

Most of the essay is given over to a detailed argument, or series of connected arguments, on WMD inspections in Iraq. The writers note, "The inspections process on which we are to embark is a trap. It may well be one that this powerful and determined president can get out of, but it is a trap nonetheless" (praise again). Indeed, one of the most disturbing features of the current process is the extent to which it takes control of American foreign policy out of President Bush's hands and puts it in the hands of people who, to put it mildly, have no interest in furthering President Bush's goal of regime change in Iraq.

Kagan and Kristol take it upon themselves to do a thorough "chessboard analysis" of every possible move by the UN inspectors, Saddam, President Bush, and leaders in Europe. The authors write of possible consequences of all moves and countermoves.

But as actions play out, say the authors, we know the "minute Bush sees something he doesn't like, he will take action. We trust this will indeed be the administration's approach"— praising again.

Kagan is a gifted writer with the rhetorical ability to change "the dress of his thoughts" from task to task. The character and style of his writing range from the direct appeal—openly hortatory and common to neoconservative campaign writing—to works of literary value. And, incidentally, one learns in studying Robert

Kagan's rhetorical usages that he distinguishes between the two, i.e., he considers it proper to tell lies in shaping common messages but improper for the more literary statement. This seeming standard of quality may amount to hoped-for literary permanency, vs. immediate rhetorical need.

His elegant *Of Power and Paradise* was published in 2003 as a book that remained on the *New York Times* best-seller list for weeks. It was translated into twenty-five languages, with its popularity extending to Canada and all parts of Europe. Henry Kissinger was ecstatic about *Of Power and Paradise*: "I consider this one of those seminal treatises without which any discussion of European-American relations would be incomplete and which will shape that discussion for years to come" (Kissinger, [praise]). The brilliant book did excite controversy and rebuttal, e.g., in John Fonte's long critical response. Fonte writes,

> For all its skill, erudition, reasoned argument (and ironic thrusts sure to delight American readers), Kagan's essay is ultimately unsatisfying. It stops short of examining and, more significantly, obfuscates the core ideological problems

facing the West—the problems of democracy, self-government, and the fate of the liberal-democratic nation-state." (Fonte)

William Kristol was born in 1952 in New York City; he earned an AB degree at Harvard College in 1973, graduating magna cum laude. He earned a PhD at Harvard University in 1979. Certain biographical facts appearing above reflect his association with Robert Kagan.

His father, Irving Kristol, was famous as a builder of neoconservative groundwork, an essayist, and a founder of several conservative magazines. See the reference to Irving Kristol in Chapter 1.

William Kristol was chief of staff to Vice President Dan Quayle from 1989 to 1993 and to Secretary of Education William Bennett under President Reagan. He supported Senator John McCain's 2000 presidential campaign.

He taught at the University of Pennsylvania and the Kennedy School of Government at Harvard.

Mr. Kristol has written several books, often with a partner—*Present Dangers* in 2000 with Robert Kagan; *The Future is Now: America Confronts the New Genetics* in 2002 with Eric Cohen; and *The War Over Iraq*, 2003, with Lawrence Kaplan.

For ten years, until 2013, Kristol was a regular panelist on *Fox News Sunday*. He appeared on ABC for several years, starting in 1996, and was a columnist for the *New York Times*.

In 1997, he and Robert Kagan cofounded the Project for the New American Century, an influential think tank and one of the first to take a stance on removing Saddam Hussein from power in Iraq.

When the Republicans won both the House and Senate in 1994, William Kristol and fellow conservative John Podhoretz founded *The Weekly Standard*, which became a forceful neoconservative voice. Always combative and leading the fight, the *Weekly Standard* was a leading publication in promoting the invasion of Iraq. Its front page seemed always to generate excitement. In May of 2003, *Weekly Standard* writer Matt Labash characterized—joyously—the magazine's innovative approach and spirit.

> We've created this cottage industry in
> which it pays to be un-objective. It pays to
> be subjective as much as possible. It's a
> great way to have your cake and eat it too.
> Criticize other people for not being
> objective. Be as subjective as you want.
> It's a great little racket. I'm glad we found
> it actually. ("Interview")

William Kristol, an unrelenting advocate of attacking Iraq, joined with others in 1998 in composing a letter to President Clinton, detailing the menace posed by Saddam Hussein.

> The only acceptable strategy is one that
> eliminates the possibility that Iraq will be
> able to use or threaten to use weapons of
> mass destruction. In the near term, this
> means a [US] willingness to undertake
> military action as diplomacy is clearly
> failing. In the long term, it means
> removing Saddam Hussein and his regime
> from power. That now needs to become the
> aim of American foreign policy. (PNAC,
> "Open Letter")

On the day after the invasion, Kristol loudly applauded the decision to invade Iraq, and again on March 28, 2003. He confidently predicted a victory in two months (C-SPAN, "Wrong Again," *YouTube*).

That event occurred fewer than seven years after William Kristol and Robert Kagan's "Toward a Neo-Reaganite Foreign Policy" was published in *Foreign Affairs* in 1996. Their famous essay introduced the American role of exercising a "benevolent global hegemony" in foreign policy to replace the "tepid consensus." Kristol and Kagan's change was welcomed by the neoconservative persuasion. Proposed unrivalled international power became identified as central to the US mission (Heilbrunn 213–227).

"On steroids"

Michael Ledeen was born in 1941 in Los Angeles. His BA is from Pomona College. At the University of Wisconsin he earned an MA and a PhD in European history and philosophy.

From 1981 to 1986, he was a consultant to three US government entities: the National Security Council, the Department of State, and the Department of Defense. As a consultant to Robert McFarlane of the National Security Council, he was resolutely involved in the Iran-Contra affair. He held the Freedom Scholar chair at the American Enterprise Institute.

Ledeen is a founding member of the powerful Jewish Institute for National Security Affairs—JINSA.

He was an enthusiastic advocate of attacking Iraq (and most of its neighbors), believing that peace could be achieved only through victory at war. In 2002, Ledeen answered an opponent's fear that war in Iraq would create a "cauldron." The comment illustrates one of his colorful ways of presenting ideas. Note the forthright irony and brash attitude:

> One only hopes that we turn the region into a cauldron, and faster, please. If ever there were a region that richly deserved being cauldronized, it is the Middle East today. If we wage the war effectively, we will bring down the terror regimes in Iraq, Iran, and Syria...." (Ledeen, "Scowcroft")

As a political analyst and advocate, he wrote for the *Wall Street Journal, National Review, New Republic,* and *Washington Quarterly.* In the American Enterprise Institute publications, the *Jewish World Review* and the *National Review Online,* he wrote scores of short jabs calling for war with Iran, Iraq, and Syria while profiling "ugly" enemy figures. Among the many other venues where he has made appearances to promote favorite causes are Fox News, the PBS *NewsHour*, and *Larry King Live*.

He was the author of a number of books relating to subjects mentioned above. An example is his *Tocqueville on American Character*, which is a twisting of the great Frenchman's observations into self-serving arguments, misusing his source. Kirkus limits its review of this book to one line: "A simplistic polemic that reduces de Tocqueville to jingoistic sloganeering" (Kirkus Reviews).

Jacob Heilbrunn once called Michael Ledeen's extremist writing, "neoconservatism on steroids" (Heilbrunn 219).

No Holds Barred

Daniel Pipes, profiled in Chapter 3 and referred to several times in the foregoing chapters, supported many think tanks and led the Middle East Forum.

He built up an enviable background in Islamic scholarship: history, literature, philosophy, and languages. Starting in his 30s, he wrote steadily, and after 9/11, without respite. He wrote twelve books and thousands of articles, many translated into some thirty-eight languages, reportedly. His work has been published in the *Los Angeles Times*, *New York Times*, *Wall Street Journal*, and *Washington Post* newspapers and many other publications, e.g., the *Atlantic Monthly*, *Commentary*, *Foreign Affairs*, *Harper's*, *National Review*, *New Republic*, *Time*, and *Weekly Standard*.

No neoconservative was a more prolific writer than Daniel Pipes.

For decades Daniel Pipes has written about Islam and Muslims, addressing points in history, sociology and culture, militancy, and so forth. In numbers of essays, Pipes laid out what he held to be the "dangers of militant Islam" (see, e.g., "MUSLIM INTERNMENT" and "Japanese Internment"). To call them "statements of disapproval" would be euphemistic, for the bulk is contemptuous; most is polemical, some offensive. The following statement is an example of his concerns—and unique style:

> Drawn to pornography like moths to
> light, Islamists integrate dirty pictures
> even into their terrorism. In one case,

US law-enforcement officials found
that a wide variety of Islamist
organizations—Osama bin Laden's,
Hamas, Hizbullah, and others—had
placed encrypted information such as
maps, photographs, and instructions
within the X-rated pictures on
pornographic Web sites. (Pipes,
"Islamists")

Though varying in approach to an essay,
his purpose was to alert Americans to the
imminent danger to their welfare: Islamic
nations are an insidious power in the Middle
East; they do not make good neighbors.
Behaviorally, they are depraved, not like
Westerners.

In the cause for big changes in the Middle
East, Pipes chose the exploration of Muslim-
Islamic issues as his *métier.* Further, he chose to
be Paul Revere in alerting the people of the
Western world, directly the people of the US and
Israel, of the "menace." Pipes made thousands of
rhetorical gallops of alarm; "The Muslims Are
Coming!" he shouted ("The Muslims Are Coming!
The Muslims Are Coming!").

Most likely, "The Muslims Are Coming!" is the work of Daniel Pipes most often cited in books and articles. It is condemned frequently, probably for its purpose and scurrilous content.

In referring to "style," trained analysts always have dressing in mind, such as words, sentences, and figures of speech. The excerpt below, from its first publication in 1990, illustrates how style can taint a promising argument. More than that, the excerpt illustrates the inseparability of style and argument and ultimately sees discourse holistically. Dressing is a part of substance.

Pipes wrote of fears of a Muslim influx being more real than worry about a jihad.

West European societies are unprepared for the massive immigration of brown-skinned peoples cooking strange foods and not exactly maintaining Germanic standards of hygiene. Muslim immigrants bring with them a chauvinism that augurs badly for their integration into the mainstream of the European societies (Pipes, "The Muslims Are Coming!").

A sampling of his vast store of writings reveals Daniel Pipes as a supremely self-confident person. But, in his mind, did this keen observer of human behavior believe that his readers accepted his condemnation of Muslim culture? Did he care if readers were with him or not? Of course he did, and he had concrete evidence of an all-powerful assenting audience: the loud voice of generous financial supporters. Besides the individual readers of his writings, Pipes was backed by a significant number of prominent kingpins in politics and philanthropic realms, financiers who expected and got a constant output of pleading for maintenance of security in the Near East. Foundations and other groups of financial supporters donated thousands of dollars to him and his Middle East Forum. Pipes responded to their expectations with rhetorical gusto, and records show the intense and enduring financial applause.

Given Pipes' resolve and skill in persuasion, donors were generous. Available Internal Revenue records testify to this. After al-Qaeda's attack of September 11, 2001, and over the next eight years, the MEF was given over 8.8 million dollars. It fared well in subsequent years, e.g., with donations of over 4 million dollars each year. While taking in millions of dollars, the Middle East Forum, in turn, donated hundreds of thousands to supportive organizations. IRS documents reveal the generous support (Melissa Jones, "Middle East Forum").

Another word here on observance of audiences: Disapproved by opponents and moralists, Daniel Pipes was approved by sympathetic individuals and groups. Gifts of great sums to the Middle East Forum gave sure evidence of Daniel Pipes' success.

7

Two Eventful Decades

1980s

With a political victory seeming likely in the fall of 1980, Ronald Reagan had important positions to fill in his administration and turned to recruiting from the ranks of neoconservatives. At this time, neocons were still Democrats, but as neocon pioneer Jeane Kirkpatrick opined, "We are really treated quite badly by the Democratic Party"—and it could be hard to resist an offer from the next president (Lemann).

Consequently, neocons were brought into the Reagan administration. Kirkpatrick was appointed ambassador to the United Nations. Richard Perle became assistant secretary of state; Elliott Abrams, selected to advise on policy toward Central America, got involved in the Iran-Contra affair. Others ended up on defense and foreign policy advisory boards.

Irving Kristol founded *National Interest* in 1985, though not following a strict

neoconservative editorial policy in that
magazine. The *New Republic* welcomed articles
by neoconservatives in the 1980s. Many
contributed, e.g., Fred Barnes, Jeane
Kirkpatrick, Joshua Muravchik, Eric Breindel,
Irving Kristol, Michael Ledeen, Robert Kagan,
Charles Krauthammer, and Irving Howe.

But, of course, the Reagan years were not
all rosy for the neoconservatives. The
administration, working multilaterally in
international diplomacy, took realist positions
on defense policy and strategy. As always, the
neocons opposed these. The Reagan
administration sought arms control; it esteemed
uses of diplomacy; it fostered union among other
nations; Reagan defense policy allowed for the
implementation of deterrents. Then, starting in
1985, Reagan and Gorbachev enjoyed a meeting
of minds, together facing obstacles to world
peace. While initially attracted to Reagan's
doctrine, the neoconservatives came to feel
uncomfortable.

1990s

The 1990–1991 Gulf War was considered
successful, but not for neocons who wanted US
forces to move on to Baghdad and finish the job.

But a number of events did occur in the '90s that illuminated aspirations of the neoconservatives: (1) in 1992 the Defense Planning Guidance (DPG) paper was written; (2) the prescription for the future of the state of Israel was presented to Israel's new premier, Benjamin Netanyahu; (3) the Project for the New American Century brought out clear demands in 1997; (4) the PNAC sent a letter to President Bill Clinton, advising him on an immediate need to remove Saddam Hussein from power; (5) in early 1999, Paul Wolfowitz, Richard Perle, and Scooter Libby were selected as members of a group to meet with presidential hopeful George W. Bush to teach him how to be president; for example, foreign policy would be looked into; (6) the Bush election brought Richard Cheney to the administration as vice president; (7) Cheney chose I. Lewis "Scooter" Libby as chief of staff; (8) Paul Wolfowitz, long-time Cheney associate, was installed as deputy secretary of defense; and (9) another close colleague of the vice president, Donald Rumsfeld, was chosen to be secretary of defense. The 1990s saw a great increase in concerted neoconservative rhetorical activity and accomplishment. For the neocons, it was a promising decade. Now, let's look more closely at some of the subjects.

End of the First Gulf War—Hope Deferred

Actually, the first major event was an
unwelcome event for neoconservatives. With Iraq
on their minds for decades, they were
disappointed when, at the end of the Gulf War in
1991, President G.H.W. Bush declared the end
of hostilities, deciding not to attack Baghdad
(see Pfiffner and Stillman). Over the ensuing
years, neocons often looked back with regret at
what they saw as unfinished business (Frum
and Perle 16).

Defense Planning Guidance, 1992

When Dick Cheney was defense secretary for
G.H.W. Bush, the planning committee in the
Department of Defense was led by Under
Secretary of Defense Paul Wolfowitz. He, with
Scooter Libby and neoconservative colleague
Zalmay Khalilzad, took on the great task of
writing a new policy statement for the Pentagon.
Khalilzad was the principal author of their
resulting document. It was the new edition of the
"Defense Planning Guidance," or the "DPG." It
totaled forty-six pages before amendments.
Though ordinarily a rewriting of the DPG occurs
every two years, the 1992 DPG edition was the
first significant restructuring of the US defense

policy since the end of the Cold War. In the planning, leaders from outside the DoD, including Richard Perle and Albert Wohlstetter, accepted invitations to offer comment. It became known as the "Wolfowitz Doctrine," even though Wolfowitz refused to claim authorship (Mann 209; "1992 Draft Defense").

When the original draft of the DPG was leaked to the press, a great negative reaction was set off. Democrats, in particular, were opposed, given the stipulated huge increases in defense buildup, the innovative specification of superpower status, and the adoption of preemptive force as an authorized choice in settling international disputes.

James Mann reports that the final draft, written by Scooter Libby, did not tone down the radical measures; in fact, Libby managed to *increase* virulence. Nonetheless, it was accepted. Scooter was skillful in employing euphemisms and other verbal softeners to avoid rejection by edgy Democrats and budget committees.

According to the convincing interpretation of *New York Times* writer Patrick E. Tyler, the final drafting of the DPG assured that "no rival superpower is allowed to emerge in Western

Europe, Asia or the territory of the former Soviet Union." The US is obligated to maintain "the mechanisms for deterring potential competitors from even aspiring to a larger regional or global role" (Tyler).

The intensely nationalistic Secretary of Defense Dick Cheney was so pleased that he claimed it as his own and reportedly told Khalilzad, we now have "a new rationale for our role in the world" (Mann 213–215).

Libby and Khalilzad's Defense Planning Guidance paper was a remarkable production. It has to be reckoned as a major neoconservative rhetorical victory, with telling inventional usages for the future of defense planning in the US. Many of the demanding specifications of the document came to be accepted over the years. The document ultimately was incorporated into the 2002 National Intelligence Estimate, an amazing accomplishment. Credit was given to Zalmay Khalilzad and Scooter Libby for their writing abilities—as well as rhetorical skills in explaining and defending the contents (DoD, "Defense"; Mann 209–215).

A Clean Break for Israel

In 1996, a group of Americans—including Richard Perle, Douglas Feith, and David Wurmser and wife Meyrav Wurmser—drafted a paper to present to the incoming Israeli Prime Minister Benjamin Netanyahu. It was called, *A Clean Break: A New Strategy for Securing the Realm.* Seeking to influence the direction of Israel's foreign policy, the neocons put together a set of recommendations for Israel and the conservative Likud party. The advisory statement called for Israel to drop current peace proposals, e.g., the Oslo Accords and the trading "Lands for Peace" proposal. Instead, Israel must use aggressive strategies for enforcing rights in the Middle East. They urged use of words to announce, "Our claim to the land—to which we have clung for hope for 2,000 years—is legitimate and noble."

The report recommended that Israel depart from past policies of slow diplomacy and act more assertively in international affairs. In the document, the Americans also suggested that the Israeli government abandon pursuit of "comprehensive peace" with countries of the Middle East and work for "selective peace" only,

i.e., with Turkey and Jordan. In their appeal to
Netanyahu, the writers counseled that he use
the strategy of unity, emphasizing that themes
that are "familiar to the Americans...apply well
to Israel." The group counseled the Israeli
government that the process would result in a
shifting of the balance of regional power to Israel
(Perle et al.).

We see here an instance of the dual
national interest that led occasionally to
questions on identity and allegiance. Reflexively,
the neoconservatives assumed, and based their
argumentation on, the idea of the two nations
closely linked defensively—US and Israel,
fundamentally united, relating as one. Nearly all
of their writings on solutions to security
problems assumed that the two nations shared
hazards in the Middle East and that both would
benefit in putting down the alleged threat—
together.

One comes upon a significant number of
cases of neoconservatives allegedly disrespecting
national boundary lines. Moreover, instances of
American neoconservatives making classified or
secret material available to Israelis were
reported. Indictments resulted. In named public
cases, charges were eventually dropped.

The Project for the New American Century

The PNAC, formed in 1997, was a think tank founded by William Kristol and Robert Kagan. Kristol and Kagan are treated above as well-known and competent neoconservatives who served in a number of posts over the years. Kristol is founder and editor of the *Weekly Standard*, an influential neoconservative newspaper. Both were prominent neoconservatives, innovating, organizing, and writing.

The PNAC think tank advocated major augmentation of the US defense system: extension of military bases in the Middle East and parts of Asia and Europe, modernization of military forces, and a major increase in the defense budget. The radical statement of principles included such phrases as "revolution in military affairs," "reconfiguring nuclear force," a move "toward a global first-strike force," and "preserve Pax Americana." The goal is clearly imperialistic, seeking US hegemony, preventing the rise of any rival power. On June 3, 1997, twenty-five persons signed the founding statement. They were prominent neoconservatives and other national leaders with like interests. The names follow:

Elliott Abrams

Gary Bauer

William J.
Bennett

John E "Jeb"
Bush

Dick Cheney

Eliot A. Cohen

Midge Decter

Paula Dobriansky

Steve Forbes

Francis
Fukuyama

Frank Gaffney

Fred C. Ikle

Donald Kagan

Zalmay Khalilzad

I. Lewis "Scooter"
Libby

Norman
Podhoretz

J. Danforth "Dan"
Quayle

Peter W. Rodman

Aaron Friedberg

Stephen P. Rosen

Henry S. Rowen

Donald Rumsfeld

Vin Weber

George Weigel

Paul Wolfowitz

The PNAC—A Letter to President Bill Clinton

On January 26, 1998, seeking a positive response in Bill Clinton's State of the Union address on the 27th, the Project for the New American Century wrote a letter to President Clinton alleging that Saddam Hussein is producing chemical and biological weapons, that he follows a course that puts at hazard the "safety of American troops in the region" and "our friends and allies, like Israel and the moderate Arab states." The persuasive letter urged the president to "seize the opportunity to enunciate a new strategy that would secure the interests of the US and our friends and allies around the world."

It hardly needs to be added that if Saddam does acquire the capability to deliver weapons of mass destruction, as he is almost certain to do if we continue along the present course,...a significant portion of the world's supply of oil will all be put at hazard....It means removing Saddam Hussein and his regime from power. That now needs to become the aim of American foreign policy. (PNAC, "Open Letter")

Eighteen people signed the letter of 730 words: Elliott Abrams, Richard L. Armitage,

William J. Bennett, Jeffrey Bergner, John Bolton, Paula Dobriansky, Francis Fukuyama, Robert Kagan, Zalmay Khalilzad, William Kristol, Richard Perle, Peter W. Rodman, Donald Rumsfeld, William Schneider, Jr., Vin Weber, Paul Wolfowitz, R. James Woolsey, and Robert B. Zoellick. All but Armitage, Bennett, and Weber have been named as neoconservatives.

Clinton's Response

The next evening in his State of the Union Address, President Clinton was surprisingly responsive to the PNAC letter.

> Saddam Hussein has spent the better part of this decade and much of his nation's wealth not on providing for the Iraqi people but on developing nuclear, chemical and biological weapons and the missiles to deliver them....I know I speak for everyone in this chamber, Republicans and Democrats, when I say to Saddam Hussein: You cannot defy the will of the world. And when I say to him: You have used weapons of mass destruction before. We are determined to deny you the capacity to use them again.

In 1991, after the Gulf War, years before President Clinton's State of the Union speech, Iraq had abandoned WMD activity. "Immediately following the termination of hostilities in 1991,

Iraq turned over militarily significant holdings of weapons of mass destruction to the United Nations as instructed" and destroyed all remaining. No "nuclear weapons had been manufactured in Iraq" (Cleminson; Sanders).

The PNAC—A Big Pronouncement on Defense

In September 2000, the resolute Project for the New American Century published a major document of seventy pages, "Rebuilding America's Defenses," to be urged on the president, who would be elected in November. We must "exploit the revolution in military affairs"—and time is of the essence. Sadly, "the process of transformation will...likely to be a long one, absent some catastrophic and catalyzing event—*like a new Pearl Harbor.*"

The detailed body of arguments decried the weak US military and presented numerous imperatives, at times calling for exact—very specific—procedures: "MODERNIZE CURRENT US FORCES SELECTIVELY." For example, the PNAC document called for the purchase of "V-22 Osprey 'tilt-rotor' aircraft for the Marine Corps" (Donnelly). This from a private civilian group is an unusual advisement on specific weaponry.

In 1999, David Wurmser wrote *Tyranny's Ally,* subtitling his book, *America's Failure to Defeat Saddam Hussein* (Wurmser). Vehement neoconservative Wurmser built on the US failure to take advantage of an "urgent opportunity." Iraqi "despotism, the greatest, most irreconcilable threat the US can face," is not acceptable. Bringing down Saddam is critical— for the sake of America's "international prestige" and "strategic power in the Middle East." See Chapter 2 for a more complete analysis of Wurmser's book.

8

The White House

George Walker Bush

George W. Bush, son of George Herbert Walker Bush, the 41st president of the United States, was born in New Haven, Connecticut, in 1946. He graduated from Phillips Academy and earned a BA in history from Yale University in 1968 and an MBA from Harvard Business School in 1975.

During the Vietnam War, Bush served in the Texas Air National Guard, from 1968 to 1974. His military record was spotty. A Republican, he lost in an attempt to be elected to the House of Representatives in 1978; he worked in the oil industry and was part owner of the Texas Rangers baseball team. On marrying Laura Welch in 1977, he switched from the Bush family Episcopalian church to her Methodist denomination.

Texas Rangers Baseball Club

Bush spent the years 1985 to 1994 with the Texas Rangers major league baseball club as part owner. The organization capitalized on his "out-front" skills, which allowed him satisfaction in interaction with others. He was an affable person, the "public face of the team," with "co-general partner Rusty Rose" controlling the financial part (Farrey). This administrative model was available for the new president to draw on for guidance, though an identity better fit for leadership of a corporation, or perhaps university president. Obviously, structures of two such presidential jobs contrast sharply.

Governor of Texas

Texas gubernatorial candidate G. W. Bush defeated the incumbent, Democrat Ann Richards, in 1994, doubtless benefiting from public exposure as a baseball executive. He ran on a platform of four planks: to improve public education and to reform the juvenile justice system, welfare system, and the system used by injured people to sue for damages (tort laws).

As governor, "Bush advocated and signed the two largest tax cuts to date in Texas history, totaling over $3 billion." To pay for the cuts, he proposed adoption of a program of privatizing the state's social services. This proposal failed. He emphasized "local control of schools, higher standards, and a revised curriculum....Bush was seen as pro-business and a consensus-builder" (Texas State Library Archives Commission).

A Big Early Moment

In late summer of 1998, father G.H.W. Bush, at home in Kennebunkport, Maine, found himself perplexed by son George's wearisome ruminations on his political plans, especially regarding a possible run for the presidency in 2000. The father decided to step in to determine if, indeed, his son George, with beginnings as the governor of Texas, was ready for the grand challenge. Why not seek help from Condoleezza Rice, a good friend of his good friend Brent Scowcroft? "Can you come up for a visit?" he asked her. "George is going to be here, and I want you to spend some time with him." For one thing, the father was concerned over the son's big gap in knowledge, especially on foreign policy. In any event, Ms. Rice did go to Kennebunkport, where she and the son got on well, spending a satisfying couple of days in physical workouts in the gym, jogging, and talking politics (Mabry 152).

Rice was apparently satisfied with George W. Bush's potential, and a positive decision was made. Soon after that occasion, she and Paul Wolfowitz assembled a group to work with Bush on his deficiencies. The names of group members may suggest the nature of the thought to which George W. Bush would give ear: Richard Armitage, Robert Blackwill, Stephen Hadley, Richard Perle, Donald Rumsfeld, Paul Wolfowitz, Dov Zakheim, and Robert Zoellick. All had considerable experience in foreign affairs. Significantly, six were members of the Project for the New American Century. Also significantly, one of the nonmember participants in group meetings—"the most influential," it was said—was Dick Cheney (Mann 251–252).

Indeed, the chore was challenging: "to help craft policy on the hundreds of issues that face anyone who would be president" (La Ganga).

"They snuck in"

Also significant, indeed, was the procedure by which lessons were provided to the information-deficient aspirant to the presidency. Paul Wolfowitz and Richard Perle made semi-secret teaching visits to the classroom, a space in the governor's mansion in Austin. It was in late 1998 and into 1999 when these two consummate neoconservative men had the first opportunity to meet privately with their willing student. Their function was to prepare their man in the arts and crafts of US politics, to instruct and guide him for success. All three were in their 50s.

The teachers had learned from great teachers, e.g., Henry Jackson and Albert Wohlstetter. By this time in life they themselves had acquired stores of knowledge on government and had established personal philosophies of foreign relations. Moreover, they had held major federal positions. These smart, battle-tempered hawks would teach from their personal store as shaped from experience. They who have learned the way would guide accordingly.

As alleged by a source in Bush's office, longtime key Bush supporter and ready advisor, Karl Rove, "didn't want people to know what they were doing or what they were saying....They snuck in, and snuck out" (Unger, *Fall* 165–166). The sophisticated instructors and their trainee spent time together and got to know each other.

Fatefully, they would continue to meet for years, in other scenes and roles in Washington, DC.

On November 7, 2000, George Bush was declared the victor over Al Gore in a contested election for the presidency. His vice president and head of the transition team was Richard B. Cheney. Bush named Donald H. Rumsfeld as secretary of defense and Colin Powell secretary of state.

The Inaugural Speech: The Writer Prances

Born in 1964, Michael Gerson is an evangelical Christian and graduate of the highly respected Wheaton College, with the slogan "Christ and His Kingdom." His paternal grandfather was Jewish. Until 2006, he led the president's speechwriting team and also served the president as assistant for policy and strategic planning. In 2005, *Time* magazine named him as one of twenty-five most influential evangelicals in the US. Gerson is often identified as a neoconservative. Politically, he worked to promote the invasion of Iraq, as did other Christian leaders.

Government speechwriters meet with their clients in preparatory conferences to discuss content of the address, learn something of the speaker's personality, thought processes, and so forth. The writer attempts to get a feel for style, i.e., on appropriate word choice, figures, and phrasing. Certainly G.W. Bush's presidential inaugural speech of January 20, 2001, gave his chief speechwriter a marvelous opportunity to "show *his* own stuff," and he did.

Writer Michael Gerson's inaugural phrasing was not typical. He relied less on impressive figures of speech and more on a style stressing forms of *contrast*, putting images side by side, one element against another: the good and the bad, right and wrong, the old and new, "not this but that," etc. Usually, his purpose in this wording was to define or emphasize a quality or to exalt a given favorable quantity of something. Among Gerson's many examples of contrast are these: "The peaceful transfer of authority is rare in history, yet common in our country." "America has never been united by blood or birth or soil. We are bound by ideals...." "Citizens, not spectators." "To protect but not possess, to defend but not to conquer." "Embracing these ideals makes our country more, not less, American."

With these and other more common stylistic gushes, Gerson, in his own *inaugural* task as presidential speechwriter, risked drawing attention to his authorship and, therefore, away from substances of Mr. Bush's ideas.

One obvious feature of composition was the purpose of the writer to make indelible his new president's identity. At places in the address, he stated Bush's aim as a personal promise: (1) "I will work to build a single nation of justice and opportunity," and (2) "I can pledge our nation to a goal: when we see that wounded traveler on the road to Jericho, we will not pass to the other side"—this one written without clarity of reference (to the good Samaritan), perhaps said because *the speechwriter wanted to say it* and because he wanted the audience to be aware of the president's familiarity with the Christian Bible. Other similar stylistic choices of the evangelical speechwriter's motivation may be explained similarly. In the inaugural, he made several references to religion and morality.

Regarding moral behavior, he—Bush— said, "I will live and lead by these principles: to advance my convictions with civility, to serve the public interest with courage, to speak for greater justice and compassion, to call for responsibility and try to live it...I will bring the values of our history to the care of our times."

With words of Michael Gerson, George W. Bush took on a challenging load.

This inaugural speech was praised by some critics as beautifully crafted. But the substance did not seem to belong to the deliverer. The piece was an imaginative composition, which Mr. Bush "recited." Gerson wrote an essay, and so Bush let it remain. The creation became "an essay standing on its hind legs," as James Albert Winans used to say about such a presentation (Winans).

Bush stumbled only once or twice, which bespeaks much rehearsal; however, he read too fast, as though completing an assignment for a taskmaster—getting the job done as required by the rules. The stolid message did not fit the speaker: the "easy-going" interpersonal communicator ("President...2001 Inaugural Address," *YouTube*).

Facing the Music

George W. Bush came to office significantly uninformed on domains of government. Condoleezza Rice's orientation group could not fill all the gaps, so Bush had to learn on the job. Quite aware of personal deficiencies in meeting demands of the presidency—needs in experience and expertise—Bush was not afraid to admit gaps openly or to delegate authority (Brookhiser). Moreover, he was not interested in investing himself in a number of vital areas of government.

Of course, he found daily burdens to be immediate and exigent, perhaps more so than he had anticipated or was prepared to handle. With choices to make, he decided on—naturally fell to—assigning others to help him cover weak spots and areas of lesser interest to him.

Interpersonal Communication

George W. Bush possessed commendable informal speaking skills; he was gracious, seeming to take pleasure in feeling the feedback in communicative interactions. He handled casual duties with obvious ease, e.g., when he took a bullhorn in his right hand into the rubble of the demolished World Trade Center a few days after 9/11 and, while holding his left arm around the fire chief's shoulder, talked informally for a couple of minutes in praise of workers assembled there (and also not forgetting to mention mourning families): "Thank you, for making a nation proud" ("9/11 Bullhorn Speech," *YouTube*). In this impromptu speech, the president was at his communicative best. Such is evidence of his interpersonal vitality, which may also be reflected in his propensity to create nicknames for people around him: e.g., "Tiny"—for heavy Richard Armitage of the State Department; "Brother George" —George Tenet, CIA Director; "Big Time"—Dick Cheney; "Rummy"—Secretary of Defense Donald Rumsfeld; and "Wolfie"—Paul Wolfowitz.

How the Decider Decided

Calling himself a "gut player," not a "textbook player," Bush relied on his instincts, following "God's master plan" (Woodward, *Bush at War* 137).

George W. Bush reported that "decisions come pretty easy." Yes, "I know who I am. I know what I believe in" (Allen and Broder). Fancying himself as a reliable decision maker, he liked to say that it was clear who was in charge. "Questions come to my desk, and I handle them." Proudly he boasted, "I'm the decider, and I decide what's best" (Meyer, "Bush").

In 2004, PBS interviewed several people who knew well how George W. Bush made decisions. All seemed to be of one mind: that *he would consult—but not widely, and listen briefly, and then decide.* Clay Johnson, a friend who served in Bush's administrations in both places, Texas and Washington:

> He's...not one to engage people in long philosophical discussions about key issues.

Joe Allbaugh, Texas aide to the governor:

> He is the best one-minute manager I've ever been associated with. He is a fantastic delegator.

Wayne Slater, bureau chief of the *Dallas Morning News*:

> [A] key point in George Bush is that he doesn't study things in a meticulous way, [that is, with a deep] understanding of a particular problem. He pays people to understand problems, [and he trusts them to vet fully and] give him their best advice.

Paul Sadler, Texas legislator:

> [Bush decided well when he had] different viewpoints in the room....But if there's

only [one] viewpoint in the room, that's always concerned me.

Richard Clarke, former coordinator for counterterrorism in the president's administration:

> He himself says, "I don't do nuance"....He's not interested in a lot of discussion about details. He wants to know, "Where are we going, what's the bottom line, what's your recommendation, OK, let's go on." [Limiting sources, he has] a very narrow, regulated, highly regimented set of channels to get advice....He only really likes to get his information from a handful of people, and he likes to get it orally....He really needs to be reading a lot of briefing books. ("Decision Making Style")

Richard Bruce Cheney

Dick Cheney was born in Nebraska in 1941. He attended Yale University starting in 1959 and, after dropping out, enrolled at the University of Wyoming, earning a BA in 1965 and MA in 1966. He started doctoral work at the University of Wisconsin in 1966 but quit to serve as staff aide to Wisconsin Governor Warren Knowles. In

1968, he moved to Washington, DC, when granted a fellowship by the American Political Science Association to work with Congressman William Steiger. Dick Cheney was off to a life of serious politics and big business.

He was/is a Methodist. He was a football star in high school and president of the senior class. His future wife, Lynne Vincent, was homecoming queen.

In 1969, Dick Cheney got his start in national office when Don Rumsfeld took him on as aide in a position under newly elected President Richard Nixon. Cheney went on to hold a succession of government posts. He served six terms in Congress, from 1978 to 1989 and was appointed secretary of defense by President George H.W. Bush in 1989. Years in private business followed. He was elected vice president in 2000, serving with President George W. Bush for two terms.

When Bill Clinton was elected president in 1992, serving from 1993 to 2001, the unburdened Cheney occupied himself productively at the American Enterprise think tank. With the Republicans still out of power in 1995, he took a big leap to become chairman and CEO of Halliburton Company, a large petroleum-oriented company supplying engineering and construction services. He had had business experience earlier when, instead of accepting Rumsfeld's invitation to work with him at NATO in 1973, he became a vice president at Bradley Woods, a Washington, DC, investment company.

Cheney had several heart attacks over the years, the first when he was in his thirties. To his credit, he carried on, despite surgery and ever-present questions on health and longevity.

This loyal Republican from Wyoming was seen by the people as a very conservative, patriotic, persevering and dour, no-nonsense politician of the western US. He was a heavyweight: a tough opponent and staunch political enemy of liberals, resolute and hard-nosed.

Standing way over to the right side on the political continuum, he enthusiastically supported US military spending, claiming, for example, that the US had not responded adequately to the World Trade Center bombing of 1993. All incidents that threaten the sovereignty of the US must be answered. He believed that in identifying an aggressor, the people do not need "smoking gun" information, i.e., irrefutable evidence. No measures would be barred in stopping terrorism; effective means must be found (Woodward, *Plan* 30). In 1997, he joined twenty-four others in signing the initial document of the Project for the New American Century.

Cheney's morality was honored by the political right and always questioned by the left. His five draft evasions during the Vietnam War, pointed to by opponents as hypocritical behavior, did not deter his political operations.

A common view—a stereotype—of a gathering of American politicians would have Dick Cheney over in the corner, listening silently, waiting for his moment. After major comments were made, eyes of the audience would turn to Dick Cheney as he cleared his throat. Now recognized, and in a soft and quiet presence of readiness, he would squeeze out, from the left corner of his half-closed mouth, "No, gentlemen, it never happens that way...." The deference was dramatic. His ethos, Aristotle's term for credibility, was a great rhetorical asset—recognized by friendly audiences.

Bush and Cheney

Notably, even before his inauguration, George W. Bush had started talking with Dick Cheney on the matter of help with handling the presidential load and the monotonous or tedious chores. Thus, Bush called on Cheney for relief, capitalizing comfortably on the vice president's reputation and demonstrated practical wisdom. Without doubt, foreign policy was a soft area in Bush's political outfit. He lacked curiosity in policymaking and the will to tackle tough issues and accomplish change. In a word, he shied away from the heavy lifting. This new US presidency, then, became a cooperative effort of duties routinely shared. The president relied on others at his reach to manage the routine functioning of the office—with his vice president getting big assignments.

From one view, the president and vice president working hand in hand would be called a good fit for both of them; it met the goals of both. In Dick Cheney, the unfledged president got a political journeyman to help in caring for the nation's business—from one who did not want to be president. And Cheney, a committed nationalist, had a splendid opportunity to advance a prime mission of his life: to

aggrandize—make powerful—the *weak* US
Executive Office of the President. He could
accomplish that goal right there, while
succeeding in expanding the office of George W.
Bush. With Bush he would model the
enforcement of a proper definition of the office—
and get things done the while. In the extreme,
such theory smacks of an imperial vision. Dick
Cheney was an extremist.

The Open Door

From the beginning of their association, Bush
was happy with Cheney's political sagacity, and
the vice president's power became broad and
unprecedented. In sum, the presidency grew into
what has been called a Bush-Cheney "co-
presidency" (Warshaw), though never identified
as such by anyone. Not out loud.

And so, they set up conditions of their
working relationship. Cheney would be welcome
at all meetings, with the privilege of stepping in
at any point. Unlike his predecessors in office,
Cheney was given a bundle of critical areas of
responsibility to handle, e.g., intelligence and
employment of staff. He assumed a wide latitude
and authority in foreign policy and security. In
truth, the way was opened for the vice president

to "influence almost every policy discussion and decision made in the White House" (Warshaw).

And With Libby

It must be mentioned that Cheney and Scooter Libby were a package—together in all vital activities of the administration. Glenn Kessler of the *Washington Post* noted Libby's extraordinary enhancement of administrative authority. Libby was not only Cheney's chief of staff but also assistant to the president (which gave him the rank of national security adviser). The ever-present Libby was Cheney's steadfast personal attendant, guarding his flanks and assuring his man's maintenance of power. Thus, he served as "Cheney's eyes and ears in the bureaucracy—and the media"—always appreciating *secrecy*, an aim of both figures in leaving no trails (Kessler).

"I don't want to be president"

Since 2000, Dick Cheney had presented himself as a man with absolutely no interest in becoming president. And he meant it. Thus, Bush relaxed. Cheney, publically accepting his subordinate status, made it obvious that his aim was to serve the president. Savvy, constant, and loyal, he directly influenced the hiring of key "civilian" support. With Secretary of Defense

Donald Rumsfeld, Cheney brought in Douglas Feith to become No. 3, after Paul Wolfowitz, who was No. 2. Scooter Libby, whom he chose to be his chief of staff, was expected to attend all meetings, as well as decision sessions that were open to the vice president. Colloquially put, the independent kid from Wyoming who had flunked out at George Bush's alma mater—Yale University—in the early 60s, now vice president of the US, was active in filling the big posts.

Moreover, as vice president, the pragmatic Dick Cheney, late in 2002, added a scholarly dimension to his political life, while his interest in history grew and influence extended. He would hold friendly gatherings in his home at Washington's Naval Observatory, with intellectuals such as Middle East historian Bernard Lewis, who promoted the Iraq invasion and was an acquaintance and supporter of Ahmed Chalabi. Often Professor Victor Davis Hanson would be in attendance, and sometimes George Will (Heilbrunn 252).

Hanson, classicist and historian, was a writer disposed to cite the preemptive attacks as an acceptable stratagem in international conflicts. He praised an invasion of Iraq as morally just, given Arab antagonistic philosophies. Dartmouth professor Nathaniel Ward held that Hanson's acceptance of preemption stemmed from a view of cultural conditions of the Arab culture.

> The nations of the Middle East, for various reasons...have never been exposed to Enlightenment ideas of equality and liberty, and...they even view Western faith in such ideals a weakness. Accordingly, he [Hanson] said, it is only right that the West stop propping up authoritarian leaders in the region, as it did during the Cold War, and to do what should have been done there long ago: foster freedom. (Ward)

Hanson posited that a "preemptive conflict is judged to be just or unjust based on its context and its success." This student of the classics saw historical uses of preemption as moral acts, e.g., as in the Athenian expeditions against Sparta, the US invasion of Mexico—and the US incursion into Grenada in 1983 (Ward).

Cheney was so drawn to the writing of Hanson that he distributed copies of the professor's works to staff members and assigned one of his aides to consult regularly with

Hanson. One evening, as war in Iraq loomed, Hanson's *The Soul of Battle* was discussed in Cheney's home.

> The book profiled three fearsome military leaders: George Patton in World War II, William Tecumseth Sherman in the Civil War, and Epaminondas, a Theban general who had destroyed the Spartan army in ancient Greece. All three in Hanson's study were misunderstood figures. Each had been maligned during their day for employing ruthless tactics. But Hanson contended that their willingness to crush completely the armies of their enemies [except in the Theban's case] and instill fear among the indigenous population had been effective. (Isikoff 159)

Cheney, deeply impressed by the book, "viewed himself as one of those leaders"—clearly, as a general of his time (Isikoff 159).

Donald Rumsfeld, too, was enamored of Hanson's writings.

Cheney Spoke Out

On August 27, 2002, six months before the invasion, Vice President Cheney addressed the national convention of the Veterans of Foreign Wars, or VFW, in Nashville. It was an effusive discourse, to be mined for Cheney's outlook on Iraq ("Dick Cheney – VFW," *YouTube*). John McConnell was Cheney's principal speechwriter in 2002, but it is most likely that the vice president controlled firmly the contents of the VFW speech, given its extremism, e.g., regarding his supporting the strategy of preemption. He aimed to be the adroit orator, choosing the right language on this signal occasion.

Cheney talked for thirty-two minutes, spending the first five or six minutes paying warm respects to the VFW and the men and women they represent. This was an unusually long acknowledgment but fitting, given his purpose and the fact that his five draft deferments during the Vietnam War had been questioned publically. Though in his political years he had become known as a friend of the military, he made a special effort to be spotless in this talk about war—which, he held, had been under way since September 11, 2001. As a smart speaker, he took no chances with this sensitive, perceptible audience.

So, Dick Cheney worked with them, paying attention to rhetorical ethos—e.g., "We're together"; "I belong"—reminding the VFW folk of their camaraderie: "President Bush has established a veteran health task force, of which Bob Wallace [executive director of the VFW] is an influential member." He mentioned US success in Afghanistan and his own credentials as a true believer: "May I say, as a former Secretary of Defense, that I have never been more proud of the America's military."

Incidentally, a person reviewing this speech will learn by way of positive citations that the vice president is sure President Bush enjoyed high esteem among VFW members: "I know our president very well. I've worked beside him as he directed our response to the events of 9/11." Sure of agreement, he cited Bush many times, rhetorically benefiting from the connection while boosting the president's status. Moreover, Mr. Cheney wanted the audience to see the vice president as loyal to the boss.

> And I am confident that he will, as he has said he would, consult widely with the Congress and with our friends and allies before deciding upon a course of action. He welcomes the debate that has now been joined here at home, and he has made it clear to his national security team

that he wants us to participate fully in the hearings that will be held in Congress...on this vitally important issue. [*To wit—the president will welcome debate on what to do about the war "we're in."*]

Relatedly, the vice president uses the pronoun "we" much more often that "I," remembering his subordinate status.

We have met all these commitments....We must take the battle to the enemy....We have laid the foundation for....What we must not do in the face of mortal threat....We will develop and deploy....

The audience saw and heard a loyal vice president who was careful to stay inbounds on matters of concern to all. The audience perceived unity in the top leadership as well as acceptable individuality in Cheney, the representative. He was faithful yet his own person. Success with this conservative audience testified to his rhetorical acumen.

Cheney and the Neoconservatives

Certain of Dick Cheney's topics, emphases, and strategies were virtually identical to those of neoconservatives we have discussed here: Paul

Wolfowitz, Richard Perle, Douglas Feith, Scooter
Libby, et al. In the VFW speech, Cheney
displayed vividly his ultra conservative
grounding and, in so doing, demonstrated
agreement with the unified orientation of
neoconservatives. For a depiction of Vice
President Cheney's political illusion, see David
Armstrong's essay, "Dick Cheney's Song of
America" (Armstrong).

Like Neoconservatives

The vice president's similarities are significant:

1.   Like neoconservatives, Cheney assumed a
posture of war, seen in the VFW speech. He held
that "wars are never won on the defensive"; "we
will take every step necessary to make sure our
country is secure"; and "our armed services
must have every tool to answer any threat that
forms against us." That means, "any enemy
conspiring to harm America or our friends must
face a swift, a certain, and a devastating
response." And "the entire world must know that
we will take whatever action is necessary to
defend our freedom and our security ("Dick
Cheney – VFW," *YouTube*).

2.   Like neoconservatives, Cheney allowed
himself to include false statements in his

communicating, inserting unproven claims or assumptions or lies—though sometimes craftily wrought: "In this war, we've assembled a broad coalition"; "Saddam had kept inspectors in the dark about the extent of his program to mass produce VX, one of the deadliest chemicals known to man." The United Nations WMD inspectors in Iraq "missed a great deal"; "they continue to pursue the nuclear program they began so many years ago."; "Saddam...devised an elaborate program to conceal his active efforts to build chemical and biological weapons." The vice president spoke— often falsely—with absolute certainty.

> Simply stated, there is no doubt that Saddam Hussein now has weapons of mass destruction. There is no doubt he is amassing them to use against our friends, against our allies, and against us. And there is no doubt that his aggressive regional ambitions will lead him into future confrontations with his neighbors— confrontations that will involve both the weapons he has today, and the ones he will continue to develop with his oil wealth.

3.   Like neoconservatives, he rejected the common defense doctrine of *realism*, reminding listeners that, in the Cold War, old methods of diplomacy were used, e.g.,

> ...strategies of deterrence and containment. But it's a lot tougher to deter enemies who have no country to defend. And containment is not possible when dictators obtain weapons of mass destruction and are prepared to share them with terrorists who intend to inflict catastrophic casualties on the United States.

4.   Like neoconservatives, Cheney urged preemptive attacks. If we "could have preempted 9/11," we would have no doubts. For support, he quoted written words of Henry Kissinger, former secretary of state. Once a realist in international affairs, Kissinger had hardened by 2002—joining with neoconservatives in their ominous and contrived visions of menacing WMD production in Iraq.

> The imminence of proliferation of weapons of mass destruction, the huge dangers it involves, the rejection of a viable inspection system, and the demonstrated

hostility of Saddam Hussein combine to produce an imperative for preemptive action. (Kissinger, "On Intervention")

Cheney continued confidently in the VFW address: "This nation will not live at the mercy of terrorists or terror regimes," and adds,

> I am familiar with the arguments against taking action in the case of Saddam Hussein. Some concede that Saddam is evil, power hungry, and a menace—but that, until he crosses the threshold of actually possessing nuclear weapons, we should rule out any preemptive action. That logic seems to me to be deeply flawed. The argument comes down to this: yes, Saddam is as dangerous as we say he is, we just need to let him get stronger before we do anything about it.

"That's supreme foolishness," as Cheney may be paraphrased.

5.   Like neoconservatives, Cheney was certain that war is necessary to peace. He poses this argument to counter views held by some that attacking Saddam Hussein would cause even greater troubles in the Middle East: attacking him would interfere with the larger war against

terror. He believes the opposite is true, that
regime change in Iraq would bring about a
number of benefits to the region. "When the
gravest of threats are eliminated, the freedom-
loving peoples of the region will have a chance to
build on the values that can bring lasting
peace."

6.   With some neoconservatives, Cheney
vowed, "I really do believe we will be greeted as
liberators" (Reeve). He held that the Iraqis would
welcome the attackers openly. They agreed with
Ajami, the outspoken Lebanese-born supporter
of invasion: "As for the reaction of the Arab
'street,' the Middle East expert Professor Fouad
Ajami predicts that, after liberation, the streets
in Basra and Baghdad are 'sure to erupt in
joy...'" (Shatz, "Native").

Throughout his address, Cheney *named*
the specific enemy, most often by the first name:
"Saddam." Thus, in repetition, he attempted to
make the adversary an ugly beast that was
ready in his hate to hurl those secretly
developed weapons of mass destruction at
targets of the region. "Saddam has perfected the
game of cheat and retreat and is very skilled in
the art of denial and deception."

A comment on features of the vice president's delivery seems germane. His droning would have been boring to the average American audience. He rarely responded with accordant vocal variety to changes in the implicit drama of his subject matter, i.e., his vocal level was unvaried throughout. In a word, he was dull. Yet, critics in rhetoric will bear in mind the possibility that the vice president—always a man of strategy—*allowed* a sameness in expression to suggest to the audience the ordinary common sense in his content. No frills from that man ("Dick Cheney – VFW," *YouTube*). Plain truth is plainly spoken.

In conversation he could be delightful, e.g., in narrating biographical material ("Dick Cheney – A Heartbeat," *YouTube*; see also, "Unauthorized Biography," *YouTube*).

Donald Henry Rumsfeld

Don Rumsfeld was born in 1932 in Chicago. He earned a political science BA in 1954 from Princeton University, where he was a championship wrestler. He was an aviator in the US Navy.

President Gerald Ford appointed Rumsfeld to head his transition team in 1974, and

Rumsfeld hired Cheney as deputy. This was Dick Cheney's first US government job, remembered as the first Rumsfeld-Cheney hookup, one of many to come.

Later, under George W. Bush, Cheney and Rumsfeld hired a number of competent neoconservatives in staff positions, placing them in all parts of the DoD and elsewhere. Consequently, they enjoyed crucial connections to the highest levels of national authority. We have referred to these accomplished achievers earlier in this report. They included Lewis "Scooter" Libby, appointed as Cheney's chief of staff; Paul Wolfowitz, appointed as deputy secretary of defense and No. 2 in the DoD; and Douglas Feith, undersecretary of defense for policy and No. 3. Richard Perle was a member of the important Defense Policy Board. Elliott Abrams served the National Security Council as special assistant to the president for Near East and North African Affairs. John Bolton worked for the undersecretary of state for Arms Control and International Security. Faithful David Addington served Cheney as legal counsel. And so, we glimpse the character of a great political powerhouse interacting at the control center.

Adding to his first experience as secretary of defense in the '70s, Rumsfeld had developed fresh ideas on handling his reprise in 2001. He jumped right in and took over, knowing where he wanted to start. His first move was to assert control over the military leadership. "I'm the boss here; we'll do it this way now" was the core of the message directed to the brass. This abrupt entry and a cluster of imposed changes in policy startled the defense establishment. Happy with the procedures they had put in place earlier, the proud military professionals resisted, and the DoD became a place of friction. But, of course, civilian authority eventually prevailed, as it must. Donald Rumsfeld was in charge.

Though patience was not one of the new secretary's administrative virtues, decisiveness was. The swift Rumsfeld operated like a commander. Characteristically, he saw a need and went forward briskly to meet it, posthaste.

Rumsfeld's endorsement of military action against Iraq had a unique wellspring. He did not hate Saddam as much as he viewed Iraq as a captivating target. He believed Iraq's military to be weak, a perception that offered him an exciting opportunity to use some of his ideas on

reshaping aspects of the US Army. Heilbrunn
caught Rumsfeld's motivation.

> Iraq wasn't interesting to Rumsfeld in
> itself, as it was for the neoconservatives;
> he was neither a moralist nor a gentile
> "friend" of Israel; he simply saw Iraq as a
> proving ground for his own theories about
> the military. (Heilbrunn 254)

He focused his mind on reducing unit size,
altering command structures to lessen
bureaucracy and move smoothly, with greater
speed. Rumsfeld planned for a "smaller, nimbler,
and more networked military that could respond
swiftly to threats anywhere in the world"
("Timeline").

In February of 2003, Army General Eric K.
Shinseki testified in a Senate meeting, that
"several hundred thousand" troops would be
needed to secure Iraq. "Any postwar occupying
force would have to be big enough to maintain
safety in a country with ethnic tensions that
could lead to other problems." The General's
figure is grossly exaggerated, claimed Secretary
Don Rumsfeld; the required number of troops
will be closer to 100,000. Paul Wolfowitz called
Shinseki's estimate "wildly off the mark"

(Schmitt). Bush backed the cocky innovator and Wolfowitz.

Patently, Secretary of Defense Rumsfeld's professional life threw him constantly into controversy, as noted. His daily agenda took him to investigating conditions of the defense apparatus, arguing for this plan or that, managing experienced generals, and prodding news reporters, proud colleagues, aspiring subordinates, and other ambitious souls.

Rumsfeld was smart, eager, and energetic. In decades of government service, he had established ways of doing and coping. In his assignments, problems were many and the responsibility weighty, and frequently he found his authority and reputation on the line. He was a striver, "hated to lose," and, in keen intensity, came to assume some annoying patterns of behavior in interaction with others. Quirks of personality have been mentioned often by writers, most references related to choices in maintenance of authority: lying, denying, blaming, changing the subject to suppress a challenge, obfuscation, announcing that history will one day judge him kindly, a my-way-or-no-way outlook, sexism, etc. (Draper; Greenberg; Hersh, "General's Report"; Reuter).

Eager to try his hand at setting policy, Rumsfeld willingly accepted the secretary of defense post but at times stumbled in its execution. He was not awed by the generals' theories. "The man is capable of raking down all opposition and has an astonishing ability not to listen to experts," said retired Army General Barry McCaffrey, who, nevertheless, admired Rumsfeld's patriotism, ferocious intelligence, and formidable charm (R. Kaplan).

Rumsfeld and Cheney

In government on President Richard Nixon's shirttails, Don Rumsfeld in 1969 was appointed the director of the Office of Economic Opportunity. Becoming impressed with Dick Cheney's promise, he asked the newcomer to join him as special assistant. Cheney accepted, marking the beginning of a long political union. Next year, Rumsfeld was appointed as a White House counselor, and Cheney came along. When Gerald Ford appointed Rumsfeld to head his transition team in 1974, Cheney acceded to his friend's offer to be deputy. As recounted, they were together in several government positions, forming a legendary political association.

The extended and close relationship of the vice president and secretary of defense augured well for White House unity.

9

Al-Qaeda Attacked the US

9/11

On September 11, 2001, pilots trained by al-Qaeda, a well-organized terror network, hijacked four US commercial airplanes and attacked the United States by surprise, causing death and destruction. President Bush spoke to the somber nation that evening.

"Today, our nation saw evil, the very worst of human nature," but we will respond, making "no distinction between the terrorists who committed these acts and those who harbor them." His religious faith comforted him as he cited a "power greater than any of us spoken through the ages in Psalm 23: 'Even though I walk through the valley of the shadow of death, I fear no evil, for You are with me.'" He spoke to assure Americans that we are a good people who will triumph over evil (CNN, "The Night of 9-11-01," *YouTube*).

So, the Project for the New American Century got its "Pearl Harbor"—justification for invading Iraq. No matter that al-Qaeda had no relevant relations with Saddam Hussein, the neoconservative cry for his removal became louder and louder. Paul Wolfowitz and James Woolsey were two who led the way in singling out Saddam as instigator of the attack (Fallows). In the months following 9/11, Wolfowitz alone made eighty-five public statements relating to the threat posed by Saddam. Wolfowitz was "a drum that would not stop" (Lewis and Reading-Smith, "False").

Robert Kagan immediately filed an opinion statement with the *Washington Post,* titled, "We Must Fight This War."

In an article of about 600 words, writer Kagan began with a long paragraph comparing the event of September 11 with the 1941 attack by Japan on Pearl Harbor. Expediently, he borrowed an indelible word—*infamy*—from Franklin Delano Roosevelt's opening sentence of his Declaration of War speech of December 8: "Yesterday, December 7, 1941—a date which will live in infamy—the United States of America was suddenly and deliberately attacked by naval and air forces of the Empire of Japan." Kagan

announced, "September 11, 2001—the date that
will live in infamy, the day the post-Cold War era
ended, the day the world for Americans changed
utterly."

Apart from his use of that memorable
word, Kagan's remarks bear no similarity to
FDR's. Necessarily, a well-crafted message for
listeners will differ rhetorically from one for
readers, especially in effecting reception. The
listener has but one chance to understand,
while the reader can review a confusing part.
Preparing the address for the US congress—and
all the people via radio—President Roosevelt
wrote carefully—as one schooled in the art of
persuasion.

Robert Kagan's potential audience
comprised the variegated *Washington Post*
readers—the young and old, friend and foe, and
so forth. But Kagan, as usual, did not attempt to
reach the full *Post* audience. He knew his
regular readers, and he discriminated,
approaching them selectively. Therefore, only a
segment of *Post* readers appreciated his
reference to "sins of omission and commission in
the Middle East" regarding America's failure. He
did not attempt to explain all assertions or give
details. Addressing a chosen and friendly

audience—confident in his status—he continued on elliptically, choosing particular content against full predication. Indirection, he calculated, with vague and spare allusions, would suffice in fashioning his message with his sophisticated readers.

One reliable method for exploring the argumentative dynamics of the statement is to employ syllogistic analysis. Remember this famous syllogism?

All men are mortal.

Socrates is a man.

Socrates is mortal.

This is a plain and fully expressed sample of formal deductive reasoning with three premises. Undisputedly, Socrates died like everybody else. But Kagan's syllogism is not from such certainty; it is rhetorical, i.e., based on a degree of *probability*, the common situation. But, of course, as people do, Kagan argued as though he possessed the absolute truth. Reader agreement with his strategically planned argument very likely was high, given his ethos: his reputation and rhetorical competence.

Since most proposals are debatable, speakers and writers deal with unsettled ideas, drawing upon their rhetorical art in response. The stuff of their messages is the stuff of rhetorical interaction, as is evident in all public remarks of all persons—of Abraham Lincoln or Jane Doe. In their lives, all persons deal with *issues*: matters in dispute, unresolved. As we have seen, every one of the public figures mentioned in this book, from Abrams to Zoellick, was a rhetor, working with issues.

Let us now apply this rhetorical theory to the work of *Washington Post* columnist Robert Kagan, specifically to his work published on September 12, 2001. We shall see that he depended on his rhetorical acumen in reaching his audience. Of course, he did not come out with a full and certain "Socrates is mortal" kind of classic syllogism. His reasoning is necessarily *practical,* i.e., based on a rhetorical probability. He proceeded in addressing his readers, announcing, "The attacks came because the United States had failed to get a 'grip' on the Middle East."

Laid out on a syllogism, this is the fundamental thought, as expressed:

The US failed "to get a grip" on threatening Middle East activity.

The US was attacked.

As you see, Kagan stated his argument in but two premises. But he had a third. It was unstated, existing in his mind. It was his leading point, his basic assumption—his real *first* premise. We can state it this way:

If the US fails "to get a grip" on threatening Middle East activity, it will be attacked.

Why not state it all outright, Mr. Kagan? Now, he may not know enough theory to answer the question to our satisfaction, but he knew his select audience and how to reach them. He knew that they, with him, already possessed the big assumption, in their minds. Accordingly, he left it out, feeling—believing—they possessed it and would fill it in, with him. All Kagan readers who held the same idea theoretically were favorably disposed toward him—with him—and went along with him. They participated *mentally* in the reasoning and unconsciously supplied the omitted part and clinched the argument, together *with him*. In a word, Kagan did not overstate the point and instead let the readers participate in shaping it—in agreement. They came to it together. Such analysis explains effectiveness in communication, in this case persuasive communication.

Moreover, in applying the theory broadly to others in this study, we have learned that the main rhetorical argument of most neoconservatives was the same as Kagan's, in essence. The argumentation may be worded conditionally, starting with "if," as found in some other instances of neocons' persuasive messages—e.g., *If the US behavior in the Middle East is not corrected, the US will go down.*

At times, the reasoning appeared categorically, e.g., in Michael Ledeen's first premise: *The regimes of all evil Middle Eastern terrorist states must be changed.* Then an example—a name, "Iraq"—comes in the second premise of the rhetorical syllogism: *Iraq is an evil regime of the Middle East.* Here, my reader, you can supply the concluding premise. OK?

As we have noted, Richard Perle was active in addressing varied audiences—in public interviews, forums, books, periodicals, and so forth. Seeking ardently to make his point, occasionally he would repeat his main argument. Moreover, unlike Robert Kagan, Perle characteristically set out *all* premises of the argument. In a word, Perle was more given to a kind of redundancy. He was didactic, i.e., he was a teacher. Strategies vary in persuasion.

In Perle's foreword to David Wurmser's book, *Tyranny's Ally,* he constructed a rhetorical syllogism, weaving it in through a number of paragraphs. He developed his argument with all three premises, as distilled here in this restatement:

> *The US' continued toleration of "Middle Eastern despotism" will lead to "defeat."*

> *The US continues to tolerate "Middle Eastern despotism."*

> *The US will be "defeated."*

Rhetorical Theory

Robert Kagan, Richard Perle, George Bush, Dick Cheney, Donald Rumsfeld, and all the rest of us live under the *most basic law of rhetorical communication: success in interaction with others requires knowledge of the audience.* This edict constrains every rhetorical decision we make. In theoretical terms, we might surmise that, when dealing with children, one may need to give all

three premises of the fundamental reasoning of
a message: "When it is raining, we must use our
umbrellas outside; it is raining now; so, let's
take our umbrellas as we go out." In theoretical
terms, accomplished kindergarten teachers often
present their pupils with full lines of reason—
complete rhetorical syllogisms—more often than
middle-school teachers who deal with more
sophisticated people. Theoretically, the same
would hold, perhaps, for a US Peace Corps
member explaining to people in a remote village
why people should travel abroad when they have
the opportunity. Here, the reader might create a
rhetorical syllogism.

Thus, rhetorical theory deals with and
accounts for choices in communication—in all
acts of persuasion. And since a common concern
is about the future, the future does not allow for
certainty in reasoning, only conjecture. Even
when we seek the inevitable, even believe we
have it, when our argument is about the future,
we deal with probabilities and improbabilities.
And in this interactive enterprise, our readers
and listeners are the prime variables.

A Final Observation on Kagan's Art

Before closing, let's go back to Robert Kagan's
writing. Was it not ridiculous of him to say that
the attack of September 11, 2001, was "far more
awful than Pearl Harbor"? One who knows the
magnitude of naval destruction at Pearl Harbor
and the ensuing years of tough warfare in the
Pacific theatre will respond to Kagan's wild
assertion, "Are you kiddin'?" But there were
readers who appreciated the basis of Kagan's
assertion—and where he was leading them. They
knew Kagan's political orientation and purpose.
It was clear to them that he had in mind a
conception laden with much more disastrous
consequences and weightier choices than those
occasioned by the aerial bombing of warships in
Hawaii that morning.

In development of his argument, Robert
Kagan advanced the most extreme position. War
it must be, he declared, assured of the futility of
offering foreign policies that depend on uses of
détente, ordinary containment, peace proposals,
and other weak diplomatic strategies. US
adoption of such measures reveals our
ignorance and stupidity. It invites attack.
Kagan's rhetorical syllogism demanded getting a

grip on facts of international life. He argued that the moment of 9/11 was not discrete. With the event came the beginning of a new war, and wars go on and on. He argued that the grand future of the American people required conquest of all enemies. He exhorted their continuing

> with the same moral clarity and courage as our grandfathers did. Not by asking what we have done to bring on the wrath of inhuman murderers. Not by figuring out ways to reason with, or try to appease those who have spilled our blood. Not by engaging in an extended legal effort to arraign, try and convict killers, as if they were criminals and not warriors. But by doing the only thing we now can do: Go to war with those who have launched this awful war against us. (R. Kagan, "We Must Fight")

Cast in quick response to the 9/11 attack, this is a bona fide example of the neoconservative language of action, spoken by a bona fide member who knew the language as well as any living person. This is pure rhetorical art by Robert Kagan—showing his firm neoconservative aim and ethos.

Report to All Stations!

In the days and weeks following the attack,
written and spoken words in hostile response
flew to all quarters. Bush-Cheney-Rumsfeld, and
their staffs, as well as all neocons in all vital
posts in and out of government, increased the
volume and intensity of the call to action,
committing themselves from their offices, think
tanks, media hubs, public forums, and all
partisan centers. The metaphor of "report to all
stations" comes to mind, with the answering
chorus, "Yes, this is what we've been waiting
for."

President Bush gave a rousing and
patriotic speech to the full Congress on
September 20, 2001 (ABC, "Address to
Congress"), asserting that the evidence for the
attacks leads to

> a collection of loosely affiliated terrorist
> organizations known as al-Qaeda [not yet
> going along with the naming of Iraq]—
> which is to terror what the Mafia is to
> crime.

Though he held them to be Islamic extremists,
he wanted to say that Americans

respect your faith. It's practiced freely by many millions of Americans and by millions more in countries that America counts as friends. Its teachings are good and peaceful.

In this, his post-9/11 speech, Bush spoke directly to other nations: "Either you are with us or you are with the terrorists."

To assure the country that the government was meeting the danger facing the nation, he announced that he had created a new cabinet position: the Office of Homeland Security. The president concluded, "We'll meet violence with patient justice—assured of the rightness of our cause and confident of the victories to come." As we go forward, "may God grant us wisdom, and may He watch over the United States of America."

The State of the Union Address

With the passing of four months, the president— closer now to Vice President Cheney and Secretary of Defense Rumsfeld—would don heavier combat boots in his communicating. On January 29, 2002, he said, though "the state of our union has never been stronger," we are at war (as Kagan had concluded in September).

Though not with neoconservative stripes, he joined the militant chorus, naming Iraq. In the long address, he uttered a form of the idea of "terror" more than thirty times.

"Iraq continues to flaunt its hostility toward America and to support terror" ("President...State of the Union," *YouTube*). In this speech, he found the word "evil" useful, and in reference to North Korea, Iran, and Iraq, tried a new term—"axis of evil." Canadian David Frum, who had been a Bush speechwriter for about a year, coined the term "axis of hatred," but Michael Gerson liked "axis of evil" better. It is more "theological," Gerson said (Borger, "How").

The neoconservatives quickened the tempo of their wide-ranging activity, passionately determined to awaken the country to the threat of terrorism, incorrectly but strategically fixing attention on Iraq or arguing that al-Qaeda and Iraq worked together in creating terror.

10

The Office of Special Plans

Neoconservative Handiwork

A remarkable instance of the establishment of a shadow intelligence agency and its ensuing success is seen in the structuring and practices of the Office of Special Plans. It was formed to compete with the Central Intelligence Agency. "When the established agencies," e.g., CIA, "came up with nothing concrete to link Iraq with al-Qaeda," the OSP was set up and "given the task of looking more carefully" (Borger, "The Spies"). No other neocon creation worked as well in pushing he nation toward acceptance of the argument for war.

The Office of Special Plans was a system for discovering and crafting data and sending them up to the level of decision making for use by the top offices of the administration. Thus was intelligence manufactured and used to build arguments for going to war. OSP operatives also managed to block information that *opposed* invasion. Eventually the twisted arguments and evidence were sent on to think tanks, media, and all other trusty places for publicizing the assumed threat posed by Iraq. President Bush and Vice President Cheney knowingly included OSP's "cooked intelligence" in their speeches. In rhetorical terms, the OSP facilitated the *invention* of proof for going to war: phony stuff for use in persuasion.

Abram Shulsky was director of the Office of Special Plans (Hersh, "Selective Intelligence"). He earned a BA in mathematics at Cornell University and, in 1972, a PhD in political science at the University of Chicago under Leo Strauss. Shulsky roomed with Paul Wolfowitz at both universities. Shulsky is an acknowledged Straussian.

Like Richard Perle, Douglas Feith, Elliott Abrams, and Paul Wolfowitz, Shulsky was a beneficiary of his association with the master of "the Bunker," Senator Henry M. Jackson. During the Reagan administration, Shulsky was a staff member for the Senate Intelligence Committee, incidentally under old-timers and chairpersons Barry Goldwater and Daniel P. Moynihan. From that government service he went on to work for the Rand Corporation. He served in the Department of Defense under Assistant Secretary Richard Perle.

Shulsky participated in think tanks, e.g., the Project for the New American Century, Hudson Institute, and the Office of Net Assessment, a pentagon think tank. The Office of Net Assessment, an independent organization, though established within the Department of Defense, is charged with discovering and identifying for the US what appear to be emerging or future threats—often related to security—as well as turning up promising opportunities on defense (DoD, "Directive").

From his early days in government, perhaps before his active entry, Shulsky had a keen interest in the subject of intelligence. In 1999, he wrote the popular *Silent Warfare: Understanding the World of Intelligence* and was joined by Gary J. Schmitt as coauthor for all subsequent editions. The back cover announces the book as "an ideal primer on intelligence...that exposes the flaws in the conventional wisdom of the intelligence community" (Cohen).

Jerome Mellon, respected Canadian intelligence authority, was excited about the book and gave it a very favorable review: for anyone "with any degree of interest in the world of intelligence, *Silent Warfare* is undeniably the best starting point for understanding the subject" (Mellon).

An Intelligence Rival

Revamped from an older antiterrorism investigation group, the Office of Special Plans was conceived after 9/11 and installed in 2002 by the master, Paul Wolfowitz, to bolster the case to invade Iraq. The "machine" acquired piles of concocted and unreliable information, especially on WMDs being produced in Iraq. The questionable data were obtained from unreliable sources, e.g., from Iraqis in exile who told lies about seeing Saddam Hussein's WMD factories busily at work. Ably managed by neoconservatives, the OSP functioned independently. As it worked to supply material to promoters, it placed itself apart from the CIA, causing confusion and other problems.

Besides Wolfowitz, scores of government officials and individuals played parts. The intelligence specialist and doctrinaire Straussian, Abram Shulsky, skillfully directed overall workings of the apparatus. Key figures were the bright Douglas Feith, a colleague of Wolfowitz in the defense department, and ever-anxious ex-Navy Captain William Luti.

Obviously, normal processes of vetting argument and evidence by an evaluating agency were not adhered to. Ordinarily, information for the president and his administrative intimates is checked and certified as to quality. With this new procedure, Shulsky and Feith, et al., dismantled the "existing filtering process that for fifty years had been preventing the policymakers from getting bad information." They created "stovepipes to get the information they wanted directly to the top leadership" (Hersh, "Stovepipe").

Much of the twisted matter was also fed directly out to newspapers, broadcast media, and other purveyors of public information.

The OSP worked effectively from September 2002 and on into the Baghdad barrage of March 19, 2003.

An Inside View of the Bizarre

Gregory Thielmann, senior member of the State Department's intelligence bureau, tells how the OSP operators went about their work, ignoring regularly established intelligence agencies, doing it their way, picking out promising material. "They were a pretty shadowy presence....Normally when you compile an intelligence document, all the agencies get together to discuss it. The OSP was never present at any of the meetings I attended" (Thielmann; see also Borger and Follmer). It was bizarre.

Also bizarre was the relation of OSP to Israel. Israelis who came to exchange information were allowed to disregard regular admittance procedures, according to a source on duty when they visited. "Instead, they were waved in on Mr. Feith's authority without having to fill in the usual forms." The visits to exchange material "continued a long-standing relationship Mr. Feith and other Washington neoconservatives had with Israel's Likud party" (Borger, "The Spies").

Chalabi's Vital Part

A principal supplier of false intelligence was Ahmed Chalabi and his Iraqi National Congress. As an Iraqi, Chalabi was in touch with defectors. With no regard for the truth, they offered custom-made accounts on Saddam Hussein's bustling arms factories. Allegedly, the dictator was turning out chemical and biological weapons and other such arms. And it was told that he had nuclear ambitions. Chalabi assured that the OSP was kept occupied in making use of the false material.

The Telling Effect

The OSP-built false reports were disseminated widely as credible information. The nation came to be stirred to the point of accepting the tales of deadly arms in Iraq; minds of the American people were bent to entertain calls for war. We have confirmation in words of Seymour Hersh: OSP operatives "produced a skein of intelligence reviews that have helped to shape public opinion and American policy toward Iraq" ("Selective Intelligence"). Hersh went on:

> [In] polls taken in the fall of 2002 on the question of Iraq's participation in 9/11, over 50% believed it. In a February 2003 poll—five or six months after inception of the Office of Special Plans—72% of Americans believed it likely that Saddam Hussein was involved in 9/11[see Gallup]. Given the OSP's scope and reach and its

dominance of the CIA, its utility is obvious.

The Office of Special Plans did its part and was inactivated in June of 2003.

Meanwhile

As talk of war continued, the people were told not to worry; the invasion would be a "cakewalk" (Adelman). Our troops would be "greeted as liberators" (Reeve). The job in Iraq would not last long: "Five days or five weeks or five months, but it certainly isn't going to last any longer than that," assured Secretary of Defense Rumsfeld (Esterbrook).

11

Cohesion

Locating Unity

An old saying affirms, "Where there are two Jews there will be three opinions." Yet, back in 1974, Norman Podhoretz found otherwise. "We are now in agreement," he happily announced. Ever since October 1973, with "the outbreak of the Yom Kippur War, it has become clearer and clearer that something new has happened to the Jews of America; they have all been converted to Zionism" (Podhoretz)—that is, they support the state of Israel.

He closed his witty and ironic essay, saying, "All by now have been so thoroughly and passionately and unequivocally converted." The ever-enthusiastic Podhoretz was indulging in hyperbole with his unbelievable projections and wishful fantasy. But his spirit had greater meaning when applied to the neoconservative cohort. All were keen advocates of security for

Israel—and, accordingly, increasingly willing to argue their cause publically.

Norman Podhoretz's sweeping assertion of the spreading of Zionism as common ground for believers—certainly neoconservatives—comes at the beginning of the time period of this study, the '70s. The neoconservatives who are featured here ultimately took their Zionistic conviction to a new level of activism. They advanced the cause beyond the pioneering resolve of Irving Kristol and Gertrude Himmelfarb (father and mother of William Kristol), Donald Kagan (father of Robert and Frederick), Richard Pipes (father of Daniel), and of Podhoretz himself (father of John). The younger neocons were out front, leading the way during the Zionistic rising and the big "conversion" that Norman Podhoretz only dreamed about. They were smart and eloquent, working unstintingly and writing unsparingly in think tanks, sending their works to the pages of *Commentary,* where editor Norman Podhoretz gave them their head. Of greatest significance in all their efforts was their accord and unity in an unrelenting shared support and dedication to the future of Israel (Heilbrunn 69; M. Friedman ch. 6; Ginsberg, *Fatal* ch. 5; Alterman, "Can We Talk?").

Neocons Flourish in Consubstantiality

The neoconservative story is about persuasion, brilliance of intellect and focus, persistence and memory—and *being together in strength.*

More than mere sociability, more than ordinary camaraderie, the close association was a singular unity of purpose in neoconservative endeavors. They enjoyed uncommon dedication—bonding and trust (see Shavit). Again, such was the state that Norman Podhoretz wanted for all. That is to say, neoconservatives came to flourish in *consubstantiality*, in harmony with their brothers and sisters: in interactive identification in *belonging, being with, working together, struggling together.* They recognized and were sensitive to the lore of common memories and current political situations and moments. In the incorporation of this spirit, the welcome message—treasured substance—of Leo Strauss played a persuasive role.

Thus, they capitalized on available structures of effectiveness in kinship, cultural truths, and accommodations, providing connections and authority. A condition of cohesion can be the most potent element in any interaction. It can challenge a negative force or ideological assault. For the neoconservatives, the use of the advantage of *together* was awesome. In this rhetorical phenomenon we locate the prime "secret" of their relating effectively as a unit—their intragroup identification. Transcending any individual limitations, these idealistic, fully motivated neoconservatives acted "upon themselves," achieving a kind of purification of purpose (see Burke "Rhetoric— Old and New").

Consubstantiality is the prime desideratum—the sought condition, the happiest circumstance in rhetorical interaction, in communication and persuasion. It occurs when separate beings—individuals—become deeply *united* through recognition of shared beliefs, values, specific elements of kinship, goals, etcetera (see Burke, *A Rhetoric of Motives*, passim; Barrett, *Rhetoric and Civility* 6–8, 29).

The neoconservative political story, beginning in the '70s, is replete with instances of cohesion manifested in acts of assisting and supporting, helping one another. An obvious example is the lead-up to Douglas Feith's reaching the top rings in the DoD. Stephen Green reported it this way:

The principals have...assisted each other
down through the years. Frequently. In
1973 Richard Perle used his (and Senator
Henry "Scoop" Jackson's) influence as a
senior staff member of the Senate Armed
Services Committee to help Wolfowitz
obtain a job with the Arms Control and
Disarmament Agency. In 1982, Perle hired
Feith in ISP [International Security Policy]
as his Special Counsel, and then as
Deputy Assistant Secretary for
Negotiations Policy. In 2001, DoD Deputy
Secretary Wolfowitz helped Feith obtain
his appointment as Undersecretary for
Policy. Feith then appointed Perle as
chairman of the Defense Policy Board.
(Green)

With a practical system that she developed
in observation of people relating successfully,
anthropologist Janine R. Wedel learned about
the critical interactions of the neocons—e.g., of
Wolfowitz, Perle, and Feith, "quietly boosting one
another, promoting one another for influential
positions, and covering for one another" and
bailing "each other out of trouble"—involved
together in reaching for the invasion of Iraq.
Perle, engaging in both business and politics,
"would actively work to help anybody he had

worked with and liked and…thought was useful to the overall cause" (Wedel 153).

This current study, too, found many instances of vital teamwork in high levels of the federal government. Such finesse brings to mind the recurring line from Franklin Pierce Adams's poem, "From Tinker to Evers to Chance," celebrating baseball's Chicago Cubs' teamwork in executing a double play. In neoconservative interaction, it was Shulsky to Feith to Wolfowitz (Rumsfeld's deputy) or Shulsky to Feith to Libby (Cheney's chief).

Forms of togetherness may be familial or cultural. Jim Lobe notes that in family relations and other long-kept social connections, William Kristol, Norman Podhoretz, Elliott Abrams, and Robert Kagan are all die-hard war hawks, yes, but "they are also part of one big neoconservative family," an "extended clan of spouses, children, and friends who have known each other for generations" (Lobe, "All"). They take advantage of connections, using them strategically.

Extended familiarity and unity are impressive as one reads instances of marriages, family structures, social preferences, and so on, among persons identified as neoconservatives (see also, Heilbrunn 107–108). Seymour Hersh suggests that the cooperative spirit that often we observe is Straussian. Vincent Cannistraro knew of the great force. Group members reinforce each other; they all work together. This has been going on for decades, but they came to coalesce deeply. September 11th gave them the opportunity, and they were ecstatic in their promotional work. Cannistraro was connected to Abram Shulsky when they worked together at a think tank: "Abe is very gentle and slow to anger, with a sense of irony. But his politics were typical for his group—the Straussian view." The *spirit* of the old Chicago philosopher prevailed in unity (Hersh, *Chain* 221). Solidarity is an apt word to name the condition.

They Knew They Were Right is the title that Jacob Heilbrunn gave to his outstanding book on neoconservatism. Being right—being right *together*—was basic to their active behavior, and it was their strength. It was necessary to their purpose, to the order—to the *persuasion,* as conceived by Irving Kristol (*Neoconservatism* and *Neoconservative Persuasion*).

Rarely—if ever—in American campaign history has cohesion been found to be as positive an influence on outcome as the effort of the neocons in coming together and uniting with the US administration to promote the invasion of Iraq. In subsequent chapters, we will revisit their combined artistry in execution and provide more on their sterling example.

12

The Invasion

The Bush Ultimatum

On March 17, 2003, President George W. Bush, via a fifteen-minute television address to his "fellow citizens," issued an ultimatum to Iraq: "Saddam Hussein and his sons must leave Iraq within 48 hours. Their refusal to do so will result in military conflict, commenced at a time of our choosing" ("George W. Bush – Ultimatum," *YouTube*).

Clearly, the primary audience of the president's speech were television viewers in the US and throughout the world, his chief goal being to justify an invasion of Iraq. He began with an eight-minute dramatic description of Saddam Hussein's "deceit and cruelty" and evil intent.

The full brief is familiar, presented over and over in the preceding months in promotional statements of the neoconservatives, Dick Cheney's speaking, and speeches of the

president himself. Secretary of Defense Don
Rumsfeld did less speechmaking than other
leaders.

The president recounted that diplomacy
had not worked in dealing with the Iraqi leader—
nor had efforts of the United Nations, he swore.
"No nation can possibly claim that Iraq has
disarmed. And it will not disarm as long as
Saddam Hussein holds power." Therefore, we
must strike. The benefits will be great: the US
and all free nations will become secure; the
world will know peace.

> Many Iraqis can hear me tonight in a
> translated radio broadcast
> [simultaneously?], and I have a message
> for them. If we must begin a military
> campaign, it will be directed against the
> lawless men who rule your country and
> not against you. As our coalition takes
> away their power, we will deliver the food
> and medicine you need. We will tear down
> the apparatus of terror, and we will help
> you to build a new Iraq that is prosperous
> and free. In a free Iraq, there will be no
> more wars of aggression against your
> neighbors, no more poison factories, no
> more executions of dissidents, no more

torture chambers and rape rooms. The
tyrant will soon be gone. The day of your
liberation is near.

And to the Iraqi military, Bush assured:

It is not too late for the Iraqi military to act
with honor and protect your country by
permitting the peaceful entry of coalition
forces to eliminate weapons of mass
destruction. Our forces will give Iraqi
military units clear instructions on actions
they can take to avoid being attacked and
destroyed. I urge every member of the Iraqi
military and intelligence services, if war
comes, do not fight for a dying regime that
is not worth your own life.

Iraqis, be warned...

...your fate will depend on your action. Do
not destroy oil wells, a source of wealth
that belongs to the Iraqi people. Do not
obey any command to use weapons of
mass destruction against anyone,
including the Iraqi people. War crimes will
be prosecuted. War criminals will be
punished. And it will be no defense to say,
"I was just following orders." ("George W.
Bush - Ultimatum," *YouTube*)

The decent Iraqi people will be free: "The
day of your liberation is near." Thus, the
president wanted to convince all that America, a
good country, must take this military action—to
wit, "you can see why we gotta do it, folks."
Bush has never clarified publically his reference
to the existence of poison factories, torture
chambers, and rape rooms in Saddam's Iraq.

Bush did choose false statements, while
fully aware of their being untruthful. The usual
lies, false assumptions, and contrived
justifications are obvious throughout, all heard
many times in prior months, e.g., "Intelligence
gathered by this and other governments leaves
no doubt that the Iraq regime continues to
possess and conceal some of the most lethal
weapons ever devised" (similar to Dick Cheney's
use of dishonest superlatives in his Veterans of
Foreign Wars speech of August 2002—over 6
months before); Saddam has "trained and
harbored terrorists, including operatives of al-
Qaeda"; and so on.

Concluding Observations on This Speech

It was a time to show his presidential best—a portentous moment to behave as commander of a great nation. His methods in speaking reflect his attitude toward the occasion and his presidential role. His rate was about 130 words per minute, just about right for TV viewing for the people of the US. There was minimal distraction in handling the teleprompter. Obviously, he rehearsed the speech conscientiously. We can imagine his intrapersonal admonition, i.e., advice to himself: "No big digressions, now. Show resolve. Be clear and smooth. No mistakes." He did well (helped by a forked tongue).

In delivery, the speaker was not sharp consistently in articulation, at times slurring or omitting consonants. But he sloughed off most of his Texas vocal drawl, i.e., he shortened his vowels, likely in accord with his view on the occasion's solemnity and his personal definition of formality in speaking. Bush did maintain some pronunciation trademarks. "Iraq" was pronounced with a long "I" once. In many instances, "nuclear" came out "NU cue ler" ("George W. Bush - Ultimatum," *YouTube*).

Though it was a formal speaking occasion, these
are minor matters, negative only if they called
attention away from his thought.

All in all, he performed satisfactorily,
though we have no way of addressing the
immediate reactions of Iraqis in Iraq.
Interestingly, reviewers in major American
newspapers made their comments with Bush's
English speaking in mind. Given the linguistic
variety represented among Iraqis, e.g., Arabic,
Kurdish, Aramaic languages, etc., the job of
criticizing a translation would be monumental.

Unity and Success

On March 19, 2003, one persuasive colluding
unit, the powerful neocons, stepped back. They
had done their part.

The leadership unit, also cohesive,
gathered in the Situation Room of the West
Wing. President Bush, the decider, polled the
leaders, checking to see if all was a "go." The
National Security Council had no further
comment to offer. The top generals and Vice
Admirable Keating, from their assigned stations,
responded affirmatively: "We are ready." Finally,
Commander in Chief, General Tommy Franks,

reported from his forward position in Saudi Arabia, "The force is ready to go, Mr. President." Then the President delivered his prepared piece forthrightly.

> For the peace of the world and the benefit and freedom of the Iraqi people, I hereby give the order to execute Operation Iraqi Freedom. May God bless the troops.

> Then, in a hand salute, with tears appearing, he cheered the team on: "Let's win it" (Woodward, *Plan* 379).

Practical Cooperation

The United States could not have prepared adequately for the invasion of Iraq without the colossal promotion by the neoconservative bloc, as led by Wolfowitz, Libby, and Feith, et. al (Shavit; Heilbrunn 21; Mearsheimer and Walt 231–234). Moreover, the United States could not have invaded Iraq without the leadership of the Bush-Cheney-Rumsfeld union—the executive bloc. The two forces shaped the opportunity, readied the people, and invaded Iraq.

Success

The massive military operation was carried off
capably, with no apparent miscues. All the world
saw the kickoff on TV, the pyrotechnic display of
bomb blasts illuminating the Baghdad sky.
Many of us, in ignorance (or naiveté), could not
believe it was happening. In innocence and
ignorance, we had no knowledge of the fantastic
promotional effort under way as the war hawks
tarried adamantly in every sector of society: Wall
Street, television programming, newspaper and
magazine publication, monumental think-tank
production, all occupied in constructing and
getting out the message. Working diligently were
the slick perception-management shops and
seamless OSP. The country was unaware that it
was the subject of an artfully managed,
persuasive effort. A large number of the
American people fell for the story. That is, they
bought the whole package of imminent evil,
including the only proffered solution: violence.
The end would justify the means: an available
philosophic rationale, eagerly sought, to meet
unease. Over time we came to understand the
essentials of the drama that was played out
behind the scenes in those weeks following the
9/11 attacks.

On May 1, 2003, airborne President Bush landed dramatically on the aircraft carrier Abraham Lincoln, positioned 30 miles off of San Diego, his stage for an announcement to the world. The warrior president, and now happy cheerleader on top of that world, was received riotously by the carriers' sailors. Extraordinary pride, told by his tanned smiling face, was answered by the clamor of hundreds of officers and men and millions of television viewers.

He read a twenty-minute speech at a slow rate: 85 or 90 words per minute. Though it was delivered matter-of-factly, without noticeable vocal variation, the speech was replete with patriotic emotion, nearly half dedicated to exaltation of the accomplishment of military personnel. Over and again he praised the troops, addressing their representatives, perched all over the ship's superstructure, and people before television sets around the world.

> Major combat operations in Iraq have ended....Those we lost were last seen on duty. Their final act on this earth was to fight a great evil, and bring liberty to others.

Your courage—your willingness to face danger for your country and for each other—made this day possible. Because of you, our nation is more secure. Because of you, the tyrant has fallen, and Iraq is free.

When Iraqi civilians looked into the faces of our servicemen and -women, they saw strength, and kindness, and goodwill. When I look at the members of the United States military, I see the best of our country, and I am honored to be your commander in chief.

Though the invasion occurred two months prior to his dramatic arrival on the carrier, Bush continued to give justification for making war. He obliquely referred to reasons for hostile action and repeated several old lies and a number of misrepresentations.

Havoc

But soon, events on the ground in Iraq banished the momentary elation. The attack that started with swift precision got bogged down on the hazardous roadways of Iraq and in neighborhood streets of Baghdad. The excitement of marching smoothly forward turned into drudgery and death as Iraqi forces resisted, refusing to be quelled. Terrible news from the fields of war came to us. We began to hear reports of broken bodies, painful suffering, and death. The statistics were grim.

The ferocious infantry fighters continued as ordered, though the improvised explosive devices (IEDs) hidden along roadways and other frequently occupied places yielded maiming and killing. The policy of concealing incidences of death was implemented by the US, as the loads of caskets were flown home covertly, out of the public eye. The best light was put on other losses.

Finally, after years of suffering and sacrifice, violence began to decline. By 2007, the United States, along with its chief ally, the United Kingdom, began gradually reducing its military presence in Iraq. At long last, the formal withdrawal occurred in December of 2011 (*Encyclopaedia Britannica*). The futile conflict had gone on for over seven tragic years.

Costs

Though numbers still are not considered final, it has been reported that "war and occupation directly and indirectly claimed the lives of about a half-million Iraqis from 2003 to 2011"

(Vergano). In addition, 4,488 US service personnel died directly; 32,223 US troops were injured, not including the large number of post-traumatic stress disorder complaints to be treated. Nearly three million people lost their homes (Kelley and Ingersoll). An accounting of other coalition-member deaths shows their losses: 179 men and women from the UK and 11 from Spain.

In economic terms, the estimated US cost of the war is 2 trillion dollars (Trotta).

Moreover, the invasion interrupted efforts to address international terrorism, bringing an alarming increase in acts of terror (Stern).

Ambassador Nicholas Burns declared that the invasion was "blatantly and inexcusably wrong," a "strategic miscalculation and the single greatest blow to American power and prestige since Vietnam." Regrettably, we lost the "trust of our own people" (Burns). This book will not attempt to quantify the national loss of people's trust. Loss of trust—always unmeasurable—is a silent and tragic event in life and death.

13

Reporting to the People

The Main Partner's Investigation

In 2009, the United Kingdom, lacking sufficient scrutiny on origins and consequences relating to their participation in the invasion, commissioned an investigation. It was led by Sir John Chilcot. The resulting Chilcot report was comprehensive, twelve volumes in length and comprising 2.6 million words. Sweeping and convincing, it found that legal bases for going to the war had not been established and that peaceful alternatives to war were not tried—i.e., the war was not the last resort; Saddam had not been an immediate threat; assertions on WMDs in Iraq had not been proved (the British nation had been deceived by Prime Minister Tony Blair and associates); the British military had been catastrophically unprepared for war in Iraq; and postwar planning for the defeated desert nation was wholly inadequate—as held most English newspapers.

Tony Blair gets heavy blame, and the people of the UK continue to cry for trials on war crimes (Rozenberg). Blair has admitted to making mistakes in the *planning* of the conflict, and for that specific lapse he has said, "I express more sorrow, regret and apology that you can ever believe." But he remains convinced that the attack was justified (Mason et al.).

No US Report

The White House leaders—the president, Dick Cheney, Don Rumsfeld—have not offered a genuine apology for their part in effecting the invasion of Iraq, nor have any of the neoconservative activists. Nor have they been subjected to a useful investigation on complicity in mounting the invasion (Timm). During their lives, *all* of these mute and unrepentant souls—members of the administration and the neoconservative persuasion—expressed loyalty to the United States of America. Yet none has followed through with an adequate report on his/her doings. Both the 2005 Robb-Silberman report for the US Senate and the 2008 Senate Intelligence Committee's report treated only the subject of poor intelligence provided during the run-up to the invasion (and both reports were inadequate in doing that).

A Case

The United States has yet to conduct a full and
proper investigation of the invasion. Routinely,
when government property is lost—no matter the
extent—a full explanatory statement must be
submitted to the relevant authority. I have
evidence of that. On patrol in my jeep during
World War II, on a muddy incline in the jungle of
the southern part of the Philippine Islands in a
heavy rain, a lumber truck up ahead stalled and
silently rolled back toward my jeep. Floppy
pieces of two-inch timber crashed through the
windshield of my jeep and up against my seat.
Fortunately, I had jumped out, thus no injuries
occurred; only a crunched window of the jeep
resulted. Yet, the next day, back at camp, this
petty officer third class was ordered to appear
before Executive Officer Keegan to account for
the loss. "That's government property; you know
that we assigned it to you to handle properly.
You're liable for any losses. Now, tell me the
details!" He demanded a full report, and I
responded as ordered.

I wonder what it would have cost to
replace the windshield of a Willys jeep in1944?
The big Irish E.O. made me feel like I owed the
Seabees a thousand dollars. Looking back

though, I am pleased with Lt. j.g. Keegan's conscientious grilling of the jeep driver over loss of government property. He was doing his duty, down there in the dense jungle at the southern end of Samar.

A Report Required

We have statutes dealing with a loss of government property. Loss is to be followed by an accounting, wherever they occur. The people are owed a report in such matters. But what about the case of a failed preemptive attack on a foreign country and accompanying death and wreckage? Is not a full and adequate report mandated? Should not the Iraq debacle be revisited from top to bottom, as the British have done? Do not we, too, believe that burdens of stewardship exist, that issues of governmental trust and responsibility must be squared, that penalties from wrongful acts or negligence are required by law? Indeed, was the invasion of Iraq a wrongful act? Was it criminal as has been charged (see Boyle)?

The United States has not reviewed satisfactorily the 2003 invasion (Timm). The report of the Robb-Silberman brief inquiry, established by President Bush's executive order in 2004, missed critical topics entirely. The statement was inadequate, as was a kindred 2008 US Senate publication. Both were politically conceived shallow reports on US failures in intelligence before the invasion (see US Senate Select Committee on Intelligence, "Whether," and Commission on the Intelligence Capabilities). Both shallow reports demonstrate the extent to which political interest can rule out proper follow-up, even in instances of obvious and critical grievance.

In a democracy, the people are owed—have a right to—access of a full, step-by-step accounting of the promotion and instigation of the invasion, including personnel involved and respective motivations. The need was put aptly by a wise old man in Seattle on July 4, 2017: "With all the dying and damage done to America in Iraq, you just can't say 'whoops, we goofed' and walk away like nothin' happened. Some say, 'Shit happens. So, it's no big deal, right?'" To that senior American, war was a big deal, and he needed an explanation. He demanded the fixing of responsibility for the gross and disastrous expenditure of human life, national wealth, and loss of international respect.

Trust is vital in any interaction in any scene, big or small. In all communication, transparency is basic to trust.

A Recommendation

Because the American people remain in ignorance of the whys and wherefores of the invasion of Iraq, this study of the attack strongly urges a thorough investigation that lays out all pertinent data relative to the occurrence of the attack and analyses of all consequences. It is required for the good of the country, for the nation's health, including the maintenance of trust.

The United Kingdom's ambitious Chilcot Inquiry may offer a useful model. The UK suffered much less in the war than the US, but its wisdom on reviewing the costly event is superior.

14

Provenance of a Disaster

Evil?

Members of the George W. Bush administration
and neoconservatives used the word evil often
and broadly. And on the first page of this
document, I recalled the occasion of Paul
Wolfowitz being named an *evil* man. The
reference to Mr. Wolfowitz demanded
investigation. I knew very little about the man—
and not much on meanings of evil as a threat in
international relationships.

Yes, Paul Wolfowitz was prominent in the
drama, a central figure in an unusual thirty
years of American history. He shared center
stage with Richard Perle, Scooter Libby, Robert
Kagan, Douglas Feith, James Woolsey, Charles
Krauthammer, and William Kristol, not to
mention many active others whose mighty
energies are treated in these pages. Among these
are the indefatigable neoconservatives who
studied under Leo Strauss and all who

experienced and modeled the compelling Straussian ardor. Neoconservatives share a fascinating heritage that includes Trotskyism. At a point in history, their forerunners were Democrats who joined the battle against the Soviets and who, in the Reagan years, came out as Republicans. After fiercely opposing the USSR to its fall, they set to work in zealously imploring the nation to wake up and "catch up" defensively, to be ready to face the palpable "evil" in the world. Disciplined in purpose, they demanded that the US become militarily unrivalled, ready to use its power, even in preemptive attack.

Following the attacks of September 11, 2001, the administrative triad—the elected and appointed leadership of President George W. Bush, Vice President Dick Cheney, and Secretary of Defense Donald Rumsfeld—found oneness in vision and aim. Constancy distinguishes all three.

Bush came to the presidency a greenhorn, but he had precepts on leadership: be smart; exploit the available talent. But *never delegate the decision.* You are the chief—strong, ready to stand alone. Yours is the final word. You are *The Decider*, Mr. President.

Dick Cheney was there for Bush. He was ever-present, a godfather of White House interactions. He knew his place, when to step in, when to push, and when to wait.

Don Rumsfeld did it his way, while going along loyally with his old pal and the boss.

Ultimately, the most telling fact was the constancy of Dick Cheney's suasory and unifying presence in interactions of the triad.

The two great forces linked tight, consubstantial in resolve to trigger the preemptive attack. It was a unique moment in American history.

The provenance is manifest.

Works Consulted

Audio and Video

ABC. "George W. Bush: Address to Congress, September 20, 2001." *YouTube,* uploaded by XJNW66B, 1 April 2018, www.youtube.com/watch?v=Sr7zsgZ75FE.

CNN. "George W. Bush The Night of 9-11-01." *YouTube,* uploaded by 911 archives, 17 August 2011, www.youtube.com/watch?v=XbqCquDl4k4.

---. "9/11 Richard Perle - The Next Attack Will Be Entirely Different ...." *YouTube,* uploaded by 911InvestigationVids, 4 Dec. 2001, www.youtube.com/watch?v=yM_JPeI2WFs.

C-SPAN. "Wrong Again: Bill Kristol says Iraq War will last 2 months." *YouTube,* uploaded by ViralGarbage, 29 May 2016, www.youtube.com/watch?v=NHcSt2GDWwo.

"Dick Cheney - A Heartbeat Away." *YouTube,* uploaded by Wyoming PBS, 13 Nov. 2015, www.youtube.com/watch?v=16NqFviGvvE.

"Dick Cheney - VFW 103rd Speech." *YouTube*, uploaded by AmericanRhetoric.com, 8 April 2017, www.youtube.com/watch?v=H9LU91nWgoY.

Fox News *The O'Reilly Factor*. "Scooter Libby Speaks: 'The world is not just. And it doesn't do a lot of good to whine.'" *YouTube*, uploaded by L Brown, 7 Sept. 2010, www.youtube.com/watch?v=npfw05GjOLM.

"George W. Bush - Ultimatum to Saddam Hussein." *YouTube*, uploaded by AmericanRhetoric.com, 19 June 2011, www.youtube.com/watch?v=vr7OKqqTb_o.

"Meet Robert Kagan, PNAC co-founder [Clip]." *YouTube*, uploaded by A Very Heavy Agenda, 29 Sept. 2015, www.youtube.com/watch?v=pRV-NObl_LY.

NBC. "9/11 Meet the Press With Dick Cheney NBC September 16, 2001." *YouTube*, uploaded by 911InvestigationVids, 23 Sept. 2011, www.youtube.com/watch?v=KQBsCIaxMuM.

"9/11 Bullhorn Speech" at 9/11 site. *YouTube*, uploaded by AmericanRhetoric.com, 3 April 2009, www.youtube.com/watch?v=x7OCgMPX2mE.

"Obsession—Radical Islam." *YouTube,* uploaded by Philemon 1:3, 25 Oct. 2011, www.youtube.com/watch?v=zdnirTQVNX4.

"President George W. Bush 2001 Inaugural Address." *YouTube,* uploaded by C-SPAN, 14 Jan. 2009, www.youtube.com/watch?v=rXzgMdj5urs.

"President George W. Bush - State of the Union Address 2002." *YouTube,* uploaded by USA Patriotism!, 6 Sept. 2014, www.youtube.com/watch?v=RHxw8UFNCdo.

Strauss, Leo. "Seminar on Rhetoric," audio text. *Department of Political Science*, University of Chicago, 1964, leostrausscenter.uchicago.edu/course/aristotle-rhetoric-spring-quarter-

"Unauthorized Biography of Dick Cheney." *YouTube*, uploaded by CTV911, 22 Jan. 2011, www.youtube.com/watch?v=Cw70FV0wdT0.

"Vice President Dick Cheney Talks 'Heart' at the Nixon Library." *YouTube,* uploaded by the Richard Nixon Foundation, 20 Dec. 2013, www.youtube.com/watch?v=o4rMMgfJl14.

Warner, Margaret. "9/11 Paul Wolfowitz
Interview PBS News Hour With Jim Lehrer
September 14, 2001." *YouTube,* uploaded by
911InvestigationVids,14 Mar. 2012,
www.youtube.com/watch?v=ni4jcGhi_5w.

Wilkerson, Lawrence and Jim Lobes. "Israel's
Influence on US Foreign Policy." Uploaded by C-
SPAN, 18 Mar. 2016, www.c-
span.org/video/?406894-4/israel-us-foreign-
policy.

Books

Ahmad, Muhammad Idrees. *The Road to Iraq:
The Making of a Neoconservative War.* Edinburgh
UP, 2014.

Balint, Benjamin. *Running Commentary: The
Contentious Magazine that Transformed the
Jewish Left into the Neoconservative Right.*
PublicAffairs, 2010.

Bamford, James. *Pretext for War: 9/11, Iraq, and
the Abuse of America's Intelligence Agencies.*
Doubleday, 2004.

Barrett, Harold. *Rhetoric and Civility: Human Development, Narcissism, and the Good Audience.* State U of New York P, 1991.

Boyle, Francis A. *Breaking All the Rules: Palestine, Iraq, Iran and the Case for Impeachment.* Clarity Press, Inc., 2008.

Buchanan, Patrick J. *Where the Right Went Wrong: How Neoconservatives Subverted the Reagan Revolution and Hijacked the Bush Presidency.* St. Martins, 2005.

Burke, Kenneth. *A Rhetoric of Motives.* Prentice Hall, 1950.

Clarke, Richard A. *Against All Enemies: Inside America's War on Terror.* Free Press, 2004.

Cockburn, Alexander and Jeffery St. Clair. *End Times: The Death of the Fourth Estate.* Counterpoint LLC, 2007.

Coll, Steve. *Ghost Wars: The Secret History of the CIA, Afghanistan, and bin Laden, from the Soviet Invasion to September 10, 2001.* Penguin Books, 2004.

Corn, David. *The Lies of George W. Bush: Mastering the Politics of Deception.* Crown Publishers, 2003.

Dorrien, Gary. *Imperial Designs: Neoconservatism and the New Pax Americana.* Routledge, 2004.

Drury, Sandra B. *The Political Ideas of Leo Strauss.* St. Martin's Press, 1988.

Dubose, Lou and Jake Bernstein. *Vice: Dick Cheney and the Hijacking of the American Presidency.* Random House, 2006.

Encyclopaedia Britannica. Encyclopaedia Britannica, Inc., 2018, www.britannica.com/.

Feith, Douglas J. *War and Decision: Inside the Pentagon at the Dawn of the War on Terrorism.* Harper, 2008.

Fernández, Bélen, *The Imperial Messenger: Thomas Friedman at Work.* Verso, 2011.

Findley, Paul. *They Dare to Speak Out.* Lawrence Hill, 1989.

Friedman, Murray. *The Neoconservative Revolution: Jewish Intellectuals and the Shaping of Public Policy.* Cambridge UP, 2005.

Frum, David and Richard Perle. *An End to Evil: How to Win the War on Terror.* Random House, 2003.

Fukuyama, Francis. *America at the Crossroads: Democracy, Power, and the Neoconservative Legacy.* Yale UP, 2006.

Gellman, Barton, *Angler: The Cheney Vice Presidency.* The Penguin Press, 2008.

Gerson, Mark. *The Neoconservative Vision: From the Cold War to the Culture Wars.* Madison Books, 1996.

Ginsberg, Benjamin. *The Fatal Embrace: Jews and the State.* U of Chicago P, 1993.

---. *The Value of Violence.* Prometheus Books, 2013.

---. *The Worth of War.* Prometheus Books, 2014.

Goodman, Melvin A. *National Insecurity: The Cost of American Militarism.* City Lights Books, 2013.

Gusterson, Hugh and Catherine Besteman, editors. *The Insecure American: How We Got Here and What We Should Do About It.* U of California Press, 2010.

Halper, Stefan, and Jonathan Clarke. *American Alone: The Neo-conservatives and the Global Order*. Cambridge UP, 2004.

Heilbrunn, Jacob. *They Knew They Were Right: The Rise of the Neocons*. Doubleday, 2008.

Hersh, Seymour M. *Chain of Command: The Road from 9/11 to Abu Ghraib*. HarperCollins, 2004.

Isikoff, Michael and David Corn. *Hubris: The Inside Story of Spin, Scandal, and the Selling of the Iraq War*. Three Rivers Press, 2006.

Jaffa, Harry V. *Crisis of the House Divided: Essays on Leo Strauss and Straussianism, East and West*. Rowman & Littlefield, 2012.

Kampfner, John. *Blair's Wars*. Free Press, 2003.

Kaplan, Lawrence F. and William Kristol. *The War Over Iraq: Saddam's Tyranny and America's Mission*. Encounter Books, 2003.

Kaufman, Robert G. *Henry M. Jackson: A Life in Politics*. U of Washington P, 2000.

Kristol, Irving. *Neoconservatism: The Autobiography of an Idea*. Free Press, 1995.

---. *The Neoconservative Persuasion: Selected Essays, 1942–2009.* Basic Books, 2011.

Lampert, Lawrence. *The Enduring Importance of Leo Strauss.* U of Chicago P, 2013.

Lapham, Lewis H. *Pretension of Empire: Notes on the Criminal Folly of the Bush Administration.* The New Press, 2006.

Ledeen, Michael A. *The Iranian Time Bomb: The Mullah Zealot's Quest for Destruction.* St. Martin's Press, 2007.

Lewis, Bernard. *The Middle East: A Brief History of the Last 2000 Years.* Touchstone, 1997.

Lewis, Charles. *935 Lies: The Future of Truth and the Decline of America's Moral Integrity.* PublicAffairs, 2014.

Mabry, Marcus. *Twice As Good: Condoleezza Rice and Her Path to Power.* Rodale Press, 2007.

McClellan, Scott. *What Happened: Inside the Bush White House and Washington's Culture of Deception.* PublicAffairs, 2008.

Mann, James. *Rise of the Vulcans: The History of Bush's War Cabinet.* Penguin Books, 2004.

Mearsheimer, John J. and Stephen M. Walt. *The Israeli Lobby and U.S. Foreign Policy.* Farrar, Straus and Giroux, 2007.

Miraldi, Robert. *Seymour Hersh Scoop Artist.* U of Nebraska P, 2013.

Packer, George. *The Assassins' Gate: America in Iraq.* Farrar, Straus & Giroux, 2005.

Pfiffner, James P. and Richard J. Stillman, editors. "The Decision to Go to War with Iraq." Prepared for *Public Administration: Concepts and Cases.* 8th edition. Cengage Learning, 2005.

Prochnau, William W. and Richard W. Larsen. *A Certain Democrat: Senator Henry M. Jackson, a Political Biography.* Prentice Hall, 1972.

Ricks, Thomas E. *Fiasco: The American Military Adventure in Iraq.* Penguin Group, 2006.

Rosen, Gary. editor. *The Right War? The Conservative Debate on Iraq.* Cambridge UP, 2005.

Rothkopf, David J. *Running the World: The Inside Story of the National Security Council and the Architects of American Power.* PublicAffairs, 2005.

---. *National Insecurity: America Leadership in an Age of Fear.* PublicAffairs, 2014.

Scheer, Robert. *The Pornography of Power: How Defense Hawks Hijacked 9/11 and Weakened America.* Hachette Book Group, 2008.

Schlesinger, Robert. *White House Ghosts: Presidents and Their Speech Writers.* Simon & Schuster, 2008.

Scoblic, J. Peter. *U.S. vs. Them: How a Half Century of Conservatism Has Undermined America's Security.* Viking, 2008.

Scott, Peter Dale. *The Road to 9/11: Wealth, Empire, and the Future of America.* U of California P, 2007.

Sheppard, Eugene R. *Leo Strauss and the Politics of Exile: The Making of a Political Exile.* Brandeis UP, 2006.

Shulsky, Abram N. and Gary J. Schmitt, *Silent Warfare: Understanding the World of Intelligence.* 3rd ed., U Nebraska P, 2002.

Smith, Jean Edward. *Bush.* Simon & Schuster, 2016.

Strauss, Leo. *Natural Right and History*. U of Chicago P, 1953.

Unger, Craig. *The Fall of the House of Bush: The Untold Story of How a Band of True Believers Seized the Executive Branch, Started the Iraq War, and Still Imperils America's Future*. Scribner, 2007.

Warshaw, Shirley Anne. *The Co-Presidency of Bush and Cheney*. Stanford UP, 2009.

Wedel, Janine R. *Shadow Elite: How the World's New Power Brokers Undermine Democracy, Government, and the Free Market*. Basic Books, 2009.

Weisberg, Jacob. *The Bush Tragedy*. Simon & Schuster, 2008.

Weisman, Alan. *Prince of Darkness, Richard Perle: The Kingdom, the Power & the End of Empire in America*. Sterling, 2007.

Wheeler, Marcy. *Anatomy of Deceit: How the Bush Administration Used the Media to Sell the Iraq War and Out a Spy*. Vaster Books, 2007.

Winans, James Albert and Hoyt Hopewell Hudson. *First Course in Public Speaking.* Century, 1931.

Woodward, Bob. *Bush at War.* Simon & Schuster, 2002.

---. *Plan of Attack.* Simon & Schuster, 2004.

---. *State of Denial: Bush at War, Part III.* Simon & Schuster, 2006.

Wurmser, David. *Tyranny's Ally: America's Failure to Defeat Saddam Hussein.* The American Enterprise Institute Press, 1999.

Zuckert, Catherine H. and Michael P. Zuckert. *The Truth about Leo Strauss: Political Philosophy and American Democracy.* U of Chicago P, 2006.

Government Sources

Commission on the Intelligence Capabilities of the United States Regarding Weapons of Mass Destruction. *Report to the President of the United States.* Government Printing Office, 31 Mar. 2005, govinfo.library.unt.edu/wmd/about.html.

"Middle East Forum: Full Text of 'Form 990, Schedule A' for Fiscal Year Ending Dec. 2016." *ProPublica,* projects.propublica.org/nonprofits/organization s/237749796/201703179349305660/IRS990Sc heduleA.

Office of the Press Secretary. "President Discusses the Future of Iraq." *The White House Archives,* 28 April 2003, georgewbush-whitehouse.archives.gov/news/releases/2003/0 4/20030428-3.html.

Texas State Library Archives Commission. "Texas Governor George W. Bush: An Introduction...bulk 1995–2000." *Texas Archival Resources Online,* legacy.lib.utexas.edu/taro/tslac/40078/tsl-40078.html.

United States (US), Defense Policy Board Advisory Committee. *Charter.* Government Printing Office, [Filing Date:] 3 August 2001, webarchive.loc.gov/all/20020913030140/http:/ /www.odam.osd.mil/omp/pdf/412.pdf.

US, Department of Defense(DoD). "About the Department of Defense." Current as of 21 Jan. 2017, www.defense.gov/About-DoD. Accessed Mar. 2017.

---. *Department of Defense DIRECTIVE NUMBER 5111.11.* Government Printing Office, 22 August 2001, biotech.law.lsu.edu/blaw/dodd/corres/pdf/d51 1111_082201/d511111p.pdf.

US, Senate, Select Committee on Intelligence. *Committee Study of the Central Intelligence Agency's Detention and Interrogation Program.* Government Printing Office, 2014, www.intelligence.senate.gov/sites/default/files/press/findings-and-conclusions.pdf.

---. *U.S. Intelligence Community's Prewar Intelligence Assessments on Iraq together with Additional Views* [S. Rept. 108-301], Government Printing Office, 9 July 2004 [ordered to be printed], www.congress.gov/congressional-report/108th-congress/senate-report/301/1.

---. "Whether Public Statements Regarding Iraq by U.S. Government Officials Were Substantiated by Intelligence Information." Government Printing Office, 5 June 2008. 110th Congress 2nd Session, S. Report 110-345, www.intelligence.senate.gov/sites/default/files/publications/110345.pdf.

Vesser, Dale A., (Acting) Principal Deputy Under Secretary of Defense. "Defense Planning Guidance Section for Comment." 18 Feb. 1992. Excerpts published by *New York Times* 8 March 1992, nsarchive2.gwu.edu//nukevault/ebb245/doc03 _extract_nytedit.pdf

Grosjean v. Am. Press Co., 297 U.S. 233, 250 (1936), www.law.cornell.edu/supremecourt/text/297/2 33.

Reports

"About EMET—The Endowment for Middle East Truth." *EMET*, emetonline.org/about-emet/. Accessed May 2017.

Donnelly, Thomas (Principal Author). "REBUILDING AMERICA'S DEFENSES: Strategy, Forces and Resources for a New Century." The Project for the New American Century, Sept. 2000, www.informationclearinghouse.info/pdf/Rebuild ingAmericasDefenses.pdf.

Perle, Richard and Study Group on "A New Israeli Strategy Toward 2000." *A Clean Break: A New Strategy for Securing the Realm,* July 1996. *Reddit,* posted by u/Hakim_Slackin, 7 October 2015, www.reddit.com/r/geopolitics/comments/2gj9j6 /a_clean_break_a_new_strategy_for_securing_th e realm.

PNAC. "Statement of Principles." *The Project for the New American Century,* 3 June 1987, www.rrojasdatabank.info/pfpc/PNAC--- statement%20of%20principles.pdf.

---. "Open Letter to President Clinton." *The Project for the New American Century,* 26 Jan. 1998, www.newamericancentury.org/iraqclintonletter. htm.

Periodicals and Other

"Accidents and Incidents Involving the V-22 Osprey." *Wikipedia,* last updated 11 April 2018, en.wikipedia.org/wiki/Accidents_and_incidents_ involving_the_V-22_Osprey.

Adelman, Ken. "Cakewalk in Iraq." *Washington Post*, 13 Feb. 2002, www.washingtonpost.com/archive/opinions/20 02/02/13/cakewalk-in-iraq/cf09301c-c6c4-4f2e-8268-7c93017f5e93/?utm_term=.cd80911b8a92.

Ali, Wajahat, et al. "The Roots of the Islamophobia Network in America, Fear, Inc." *Center for American Progress*, 26 August 2011, www.americanprogress.org/issues/religion/repo rts/2011/08/26/10165/fear-inc/.

Allen, Mike and David S. Broder. "Bush's Leadership Style: Decisive or Simplistic?" *Washington Post*, 30 Aug. 2004, www.washingtonpost.com/wp-dyn/articles/A45277-2004Aug29.html.

Alterman, Eric. "Can We Talk?" *The Nation*, 3 April 2003, www.thenation.com/article/can-we-talk/.

---. The Rehabilitation of Elliott Abrams." *The Nation*, 13 Mar. 2013, www.thenation.com/article/rehabilitation-elliott-abrams/.

Armbruster, Ben. "Novak: 'I Don't Think I Hurt Valerie Plame' And I Would Out Her Again Because the Left 'Tried To Ruin Me.'" *Think Progress*, 3 Dec. 2008, thinkprogress.org/novak-i-dont-think-i-hurt-valerie-plame-and-i-would-out-her-again-because-the-left-tried-to-ruin-me-2f34f1eb9f06/.

Armstrong, David, "Dick Cheney's Song of America: Drafting a Plan for Global Dominance." *Harper's*, Oct. 2002, harpers.org/archive/2002/10/dick-cheneys-song-of-America/.

Atlas, James. "Leo-Cons; A Classicist's Legacy: New Empire Builders." *New York Times,* 4 May 2003, www.nytimes.com/2003/05/04/weekinreview/the-nation-leo-cons-a-classicist-s-legacy-new-empire-builders.html.

Auster, Lawrence. On "Leo Strauss's Traditionalist Defense of Israel" [contains the 5 Jan.1956 letter to the editors of *National Review*]. *View from the Right,* 28 June 2006, www.amnation.com/vfr/archives/005967.html.

Bacevich, Andrew. "A Letter to Paul Wolfowitz." *Harper's*, Mar. 2013, harpers.org/archive/2013/03/a-letter-to-paul-wolfowitz/.

Bamford, James. "The Man Who Sold the War." *Rolling Stone*, 18 Nov. 2005, www.rollingstone.com/music/pictures/rolling-stones-biggest-scoops-exposes-and-controversies-2-aa-624/the-man-who-sold-the-war-by-james-bamford-3323040.

Bergen, Peter. "Did One Woman's Obsession Take America to War?" *The Guardian*, 5 July 2004, www.theguardian.com/world/2004/jul/05/iraq.iraq.

Blumenthal, Sidney. "RICHARD PERLE, DISARMED BUT UNDETERRED." Washington Post, 23 Nov. 1987, www.washingtonpost.com/archive/lifestyle/1987/11/23/richard-perle-disarmed-but-undeterred/b83a9f49-8d43-41bd-8e6f-1316efd52075/?utm_term=.904ed04f7e7a.

Boot, Max. 'The Case for American Empire: The Most Realistic Response to Terrorism is for America to Embrace Its Imperial Role.*" Weekly Standard*, 15 Oct. 2001, www.weeklystandard.com/the-case-for-american-empire/article/1626.

Borger, Julian. "How I Created the Axis of Evil." *The Guardian*, 28 Jan. 2003, www.theguardian.com/world/2003/jan/28/usa .iran.

---. "The Spies Who Pushed for War." *The Guardian*, 17 July 2003, www.theguardian.com/world/2003/jul/17/iraq. usa.

Brookhiser, Richard. "Close Up: The Mind of George W. Bush." *Atlantic*, Apr. 2003, www.theatlantic.com/magazine/archive/2003/0 4/close-up-the-mind-of-george-w-bush/303399/.

Brooks, David. "Saddam's Brain." *Weekly Standard,* 11 Nov. 2002, www.weeklystandard.com/saddams-brain/article/3114.

Brown University research course. "Elliot Abrams Assistant Secretary for Inter-American Affairs." *Understanding the Iran- Contra Affairs,* www.brown.edu/Research/Understanding_the_Iran_Contra_Affair/profile-abrams.php.

Burke, Kenneth. "Rhetoric—Old and New." *Journal of General Education,* Apr. 1951.

Burns, Nicholas. "Iraq War Damaged US Credibility." *Boston Globe,* 21 Dec. 2011, www.bostonglobe.com/opinion/2011/12/21/iraq-war-damaged-credibility/CU9B64xgfdGGhzG8NTWqJL/story.html.

Burnyeat, M.F. "Sphinx Without a Secret." *New York Review of Books,* 30 May 1985, www.nybooks.com/articles/1985/05/30/sphinx-without-a-secret/#fn-4.

"Campaign Launched to Monitor Middle East Studies: 'Campus Watch' to Survey Over 250 Universities." *Middle East Forum,* 18 Sept. 2002, www.meforum.org/506/campaign-launched-to-monitor-middle-east-studies.

Chan, Sewell. "Ahmad Chalabi, Iraqi Politician Who Pushed for U.S. Invasion, Dies at 71." *New York Times*, 3 Nov. 2015, www.nytimes.com/2015/11/04/world/middleea st/ahmad-chalabi-iraq-dead.html.

"The Chilcot Report by Numbers." *The Times [of London]*, 7 July 2016, www.thetimes.co.uk/article/the-chilcot-report-by-numbers-n9t2bnl5q.

"Chilcot Report: Key Points from the Iraq Inquiry." *The Guardian*, 6 July 2016, www.theguardian.com/uk-news/2016/jul/06/iraq-inquiry-key-points-from-the-chilcot-report.

"Chilcot Report: Summary of Main Findings." *Irish Times*, 6 July 2016, www.irishtimes.com/news/world/uk/chilcot-report-summary-of-main-findings-1.2712364.

"Chronicles of Greed: Hollinger International Turns Its Guns on Its Board of Directors." *The Economist*, 2 Sept.2004, www.economist.com/node/3157783.

"Clarion Project." *Right Web*, 21 Jan. 2015, rightweb.irc-online.org/profile/clarion_fund/.

Cleminson, Frank Ronald. "What Happened to Saddam's Weapons of Mass Destruction?" *Arms Control Today*, 1 Sept. 2003, www.armscontrol.org/act/2003_09/Cleminson_09.

Cohen, Eliot A. Testimonial. *Silent Warfare: Understanding the World of Intelligence*, 3rd ed., by Shulsky and Schmitt, Potomac Books, Inc., 2002, back cover, www.amazon.com/Silent-Warfare-Understanding-World-Intelligence/dp/1574883453/ref=tmm_pap_swatch_0?_encoding=UTF8&qid=1560445878&sr=1-1-catcorr.

Cohler-Esses, Larry. "Bunkum From Benador." *The Nation*, 14 July 2006, www.thenation.com/article/bunkum-benador/.

Cole, Juan. "Feith Resigns Under Pressure of Investigations." *Informed Comment*, 28 Jan. 2005, www.juancole.com/2005/01/feith-resigns-under-pressure-of.html.

Corn, David. "Elliott Abrams: It's Back!" *The Nation*, 14 June 2001, www.thenation.com/article/elliott-abrams-its-back/.

Cornfield, Jerry. "Henry M. Jackson's Name Endures Around the Region." *HeraldNet,* 30 May 2012, www.heraldnet.com/news/henry-m-jacksons-name-endures-around-the-region/

Crowley, Michael. "From Iran-Contra to Bush's Democracy Czar." *Slate,* 17 Feb. 2005, www.slate.com/articles/news_and_politics/asse ssment/2005/02/elliott_abrams.html.

Curtiss, Richard H. "You Don't Have To Be Jewish To Be a Neocon: John Bolton and James Woolsey." Article excerpt from the *Washington Report on Middle East Affairs,* vol. 22, no. 8, Oct. 2003, *Questia,* www.questia.com/magazine/1P3-419962291/you-don-t-have-to-be-jewish-to-be-a-neocon-john-bolton.

"Daniel Pipes." *Right Web,* Oct.26 2015, rightweb.irc-online.org/profile/daniel-pipes/.

Dickerson, John. "Who Is Scooter Libby?" *Slate,* 21 Oct. 2005, www.slate.com/articles/news_and_politics/politi cs/2005/10/who_is_scooter_.html.

"Decision Making Style." PBS *Frontline,* 12 Oct. 2004,
www.pbs.org/wgbh/pages/frontline/shows/choice2004/bush/style.html.

"Dick Cheney on Defense." *On the Issues,* www.ontheissues.org/Celeb/Dick_Cheney_Defense.htm.

Dizard, John. "How Ahmed Chalabi Conned the Neocons." *Salon,* 4 May 2004, www.salon.com/2004/05/04/chalabi_4/

Draper, Robert. "And He Shall Be Judged." *GQ,* 31 May 2009, www.gq.com/story/donald-rumsfeld-administration-peers-detractors.

Drew, Elizabeth. "The Neocons in Power." *New York Review of Books,* 12 June 2003, www.nybooks.com/articles/2003/06/12/the-neocons-in-power/.

Dreyfuss, Robert. "The Pentagon Muzzles the CIA." *The American Prospect,* 21 Nov. 2002, prospect.org/article/pentagon-muzzles-cia.

Dreyfuss, Robert and Jason Vest. "The Lie Factory." *Mother Jones,* Jan./Feb. 2004, www.motherjones.com/politics/2004/01/lie-factory.

Drogin, Bob and John Goetz. "How U.S. Fell Under the Spell of 'Curveball.' *Los Angeles Times*, 20 Nov. 2017, www.latimes.com/world/middleeast/la-na-curveball20nov20-story.html.

"Elliott Abrams." *Jewish Virtual Library*, www.jewishvirtuallibrary.org/elliot-abrams.

Esterbrook, John. "Rumsfeld: It Would Be a Short War." *CBS News*, 15 Nov. 2002, www.cbsnews.com/news/rumsfeld-it-would-be-a-short-war/.

Fallows, James. "Blind Into Baghdad." *The Atlantic*, Jan./Feb. 2004, www.theatlantic.com/magazine/archive/2004/01/blind-into-baghdad/302860/.

Farrey, Tom. "Kicking Back and Getting Down to Business." *ESPN*, 2 Nov. 2000, static.espn.go.com/mlb/bush/wednesday.html.

Fawal, Richard. "What Do People Who Work for Think Tanks Do?" *The Brookings Institute*, 4 Oct. 2013, www.quora.com/What-do-people-who-work-for-think-tanks-do?share=1.

"FBI Looks at Pentagon Worker in Israel Spy Probe." *CNN.com*, 27 Aug. 2004, www.cnn.com/2004/US/08/27/fbi.spy/.

Fingerhut, Eric. "EMET Pulls Out of Involvement With 'Obsession Project.'" *JTA-The Telegraph*, 30 Sept. 2008, www.jta.org/2008/09/30/news-opinion/the-telegraph/emet-pulls-out-of-involvement-with-obsession-project.

Foer, Franklin. "Flacks Americana." *New Republic*, 19 May 2002, newrepublic.com/article/68667/flacks-americana.

Follmer, Max. "Karen Kwiatkowski: The Soldier Who Spoke Out." *Huffington Post*, 18 Mar. 2008, www.huffingtonpost.com/2008/03/18/karen-kwiatkowski-the-ol_n_92237.html.

Fonte, John D. "Critical Review of Robert Kagan's *Of Paradise and Power*." *AEI*, 7 April 2003, www.aei.org/publication/critical-review-of-robert-kagans-of-paradise-and-power/.

Friedman, Thomas L. "A Manifesto for the Fast World." *New York Times*, 28 Mar. 1999, www.nytimes.com/1999/03/28/magazine/a-manifesto-for-the-fast-world.html.

---. "Chicken à la Iraq," *New York Times*, 5 Mar. 2003, www.nytimes.com/2003/03/05/opinion/chicke n-a-la-iraq.html.

From the Editors. "The Times and Iraq." *New York Times*, 26 May 2004, www.nytimes.com/2004/05/26/world/from-the-editors-the-times-and-iraq.html.

Galloway, Joseph L. "Officials Disagree Over Number of Troops Needed in Postwar Iraq." *Knight Ridder Newspapers*, 11 Mar. 2003, www.mcclatchydc.com/latest-news/article24434299.html.

Gallup Poll Editorial Staff. "Nine Key Questions About Public Opinion on Iraq." *Gallup News Service*, 1 Oct. 2002, news.gallup.com/poll/6919/nine-key-questions-about-public-opinion-iraq.aspx.

Gerth, Jeff. "Aide Urged Pentagon to Consider Weapons Made by Former Client." *New York Times*, 17 April 1983, www.nytimes.com/1983/04/17/us/aide-urged-pentagon-to-consider-weapons-made-by-former-client.html?pagewanted=all. (See also *New York Times*, 21 April 1983).

Giraldi, Philip. "Saving Feith." *The American Conservative*, 12 Mar. 2007, www.theamericanconservative.com/articles/saving-feith/.

Goldberg, Michelle. "Taboo Truths of the Conspiracy Minded." *The Public Eye,* Summer 2009, www.publiceye.org/magazine/v24n2/book-transparent-cabal.html.

Goldstein, Amy. "Bush Commutes Libby's Prison Sentence." *Washington Post,* 3 July 2007, www.washingtonpost.com/wp-dyn/content/article/2007/07/02/AR2007070200825.html.

Goodman, Amy, "James Bamford: The Shadow Factory: The Ultra-Secret NSA from 9/11 to the Eavesdropping on America." *Democracy Now,* 14 Oct.2008, www.democracynow.org/2008/10/14/james_bamford_the_shadow_factory_the.

Goodstein, Laurie. "Threats and Responses: American Jews; Divide Among Jews Leads to Silence on Iraq War." *New York Times*, 15 Mar. 2003, www.nytimes.com/2003/03/15/world/threats-responses-american-jews-divide-among-jews-leads-silence-iraq-war.html?mcubz=3.

Gora, Tahir. "Don't Confuse Islam With Islamism." *Huffington Post*, 27 May 2013, www.huffingtonpost.ca/tahir-gora/moderate-islam_b_3314561.html.

Green, Stephen. "Neo-Cons, Israel and the Bush Administration." *Counterpunch*, 28 Feb.2004, www.counterpunch.org/2004/02/28/neo-cons-israel-and-the-bush-administration/. (*See also*, Suellentrop)

Greenberg, Karen. "What Did We Learn from Abu Ghraib?" *Mother Jones*, 28 Apr. 2014, www.motherjones.com/politics/2014/04/10-anniversary-abu-ghraib-america-torture/.

Hagan, Joe. "She's Richard Perle's Oyster." *Observer*, 7 Apr. 2003, observer.com/2003/04/shes-richard-perles-oyster/.

Hedges, Stephen J. "Firm Helps U.S. Mold News Abroad." *Chicago Tribune*, 13 Nov. 2005, articles.chicagotribune.com/2005-11-13/news/0511130330_1_rendon-group-pentagon-proponents-of-open-government/2.

Hersh, Seymour M. "The General's Report: How Antonio Taguba, Who Investigated the Abu Ghraib Scandal, Became One of Its Casualties." *New Yorker*, 26 June 2007, www.newyorker.com/magazine/2007/06/25/the-generals-report.

---. "Kissinger and Nixon in the White House." *The Atlantic*, May 1982, www.theatlantic.com/magazine/archive/1982/05/kis-singer-and-nixon-in-the-white-house/308778/.

---. "Lunch With the Chairman: Why was Richard Perle meeting with Adnan Khashoggi?" *The New Yorker*, 17 Mar 2003, www.newyorker.com/magazine/2003/03/17/lunch-with-the-chairman.

---. "Selective Intelligence." *New Yorker*, 12 May 2003, www.newyorker.com/magazine/2003/05/12/selective-intelligence.

---. "The Stovepipe: How Conflicts Between the Bush Administration and the Intelligence Community Marred the Reporting on Iraq's Weapons." *New Yorker*, 27 Oct. 2003, www.newyorker.com/magazine/2003/10/27/the-stovepipe.

"His UNdoing; America's UN Ambassador Quits." *Economist*, 7 Dec. 2006, www.economist.com/node/8382325.

"History of the Henry M. 'Scoop' Jackson Distinguished Service Award." *JINSA*, www.jinsa.org/events-programs/jackson-award-dinners/history-henry-m-scoop-jackson-distinguished-service-award.

Hitchens, Christopher. "A Tale of Two Tell-Alls." Review of *War and Decision*, by Douglas J. Feith. *Slate*, 2 June 2008, www.slate.com/articles/news_and_politics/fighting_words/2008/06/a_tale_of_two_tellalls.html.

Holmes, Jonathan. "Interview with Jim Lobe." *Inter Press Service*, 17 Feb. 2003, www.brussellstribunal.org/bios/Lobe.htm.

Horton, Scott. "Fall of the House of Bush: Six Questions for Craig Unger." *Harpers*, 19 Nov 2007, harpers.org/blog/2007/11/fall-of-the-house-of-bush-six-questions-for-craig-unger/.

Husain, Khurram. "Neocons: The Men Behind the Curtain." *Bulletin of the Atomic Scientists*, vol. 59, no. 6, 2003, pp. 62–71, thebulletin.org/2003/november/neocons-men-behind-curtain.

Hylton, Wil S. "The Big Bad Wolfowitz." *GQ*, 30 Oct. 2006, www.gq.com/story/paul-wolfowitz-iraq.

"Interview with Matt Labash." *JournalismJobs.com.*, 3 May 2003, zfacts.com/metaPage/lib/Weekly_Standard_Matt-Labash_confesses.pdf.

Jones, Jeffrey M. "Among Religious Groups, Jewish Americans Most Strongly Oppose War." *Gallup News Service*, 23 Feb. 2007, news.gallup.com/poll/26677/among-religious-groups-jewish-americans-most-strongly-oppose-war.aspx.

---. "Public Support for Iraq Invasion Inches Upward." *Gallup News Service*, 17 Mar. 2003, www.gallup.com/poll/7990/public-support-iraq-invasion-inches-upward.aspx.

Jones, Melissa. "Middle East Forum." *Powerbase*, 22 Mar. 2017, powerbase.info/index.php/Middle_East_Forum#Known_funders_over_time.

"Kagan." *Brookings Institute*, www.brookings.edu/experts/robert-kagan/.

Kagan, Frederick W. "The Threatening Storm by Kenneth M. Pollack." *Commentary*, Dec. 2002, www.commentarymagazine.com/articles/the-threatening-storm-by-kenneth-m-pollack/.

Kagan, Robert. "The Benevolent Empire." *Foreign Policy*, Summer 1998, www.kropfpolisci.com/imperialism.kagan.pdf.

---. "We Must Fight This War." *Washington Post,* 11 Sept. 2001, carnegieendowment.org/2001/09/11/we-must-fight-this-war-pub-768.

Kagan, Robert and William Kristol. "The Right War." *Weekly Standard,* 1 Oct. 2001, www.weeklystandard.com/the-right-war/article/1410.

---. "The U.N. Trap?" *Weekly Standard,* 18 Nov. 2002, www.weeklystandard.com/the-u.n.-trap/article/3158.

Kamarck, Elaine C. "The Relationship That Rules the World: Modern Presidents and Their Vice Presidents." *Center for Effective Public Management at Brookings,* Sept. 2016, www.brookings.edu/wp-content/uploads/2016/09/modern-vp-final.pdf.

Kampeas, Ron. "Charles Vanik Dies at 94." *Jewish Telegraphic Agency,* 31 Aug. 2007, www.jta.org/2007/08/31/news-opinion/politics/charles-vanik-dies-at-94.

Kaplan, Robert D. **"What Rumsfeld Got Right."** *Atlantic,* July/Aug. 2008, www.theatlantic.com/magazine/archive/2008/07/what-rumsfeld-got-right/306870/.

Kelley, Michael B. and Geoffrey Ingersoll. "The Staggering Cost of the Last Decade's US War In Iraq—In Numbers." *Business Insider*, 20 June 2014, www.businessinsider.com/the-iraq-war-by-numbers-2014-6.

Kessler, Glenn. "With Vice President, He Shaped Iraq Policy." *Washington Post*, 29 Oct. 2005, www.washingtonpost.com/wp-dyn/content/article/2005/10/28/AR20051028 02139.html.

"Khalilzad, Zalmay." *Right Web*, 1 July 2011, rightweb.irc-online.org/profile/Khalilzad_Zalmay/.

Kirchick, James. "Upset about the Iraq War? Blame Iraqis." *National Review*, 18 July 2016, www.nationalreview.com/article/437974/iraq-war-iraqs-disaster-today-can-be-blamed-iraqis-not-americans-or-brits.

Kirkus Reviews. Review of *Tocqueville on American Character*, by Michael Ledeen. 1 June 2000. *Kirkus*, posted online 20 May 2010, www.kirkusreviews.com/book-reviews/michael-a-ledeen/tocqueville-on-american-character/.

Kissinger, Henry. "On Intervention in Iraq." *Washington Post*, 12 Aug. 2002.

---. [praise within review of] *Of Paradise and Power: America and Europe in the New World Order*, by Robert Kagan. *Penguin Random House Canada*, 2004, penguinrandomhouse.ca/books/89276/paradise-and-power#9781400034185.

Krauthammer, Charles. "This Is Not Crime, This Is War." *Townhall*, 12 Sept. 2011, townhall.com/columnists/charleskrauthammer/2001/09/12/this-is-not-crime,-this-is-war-n1019058.

Kristol, Irving. "The Neoconservative Persuasion: What It Was, And What It Is." *Weekly Standard*, 25 Aug. 2003, www.weeklystandard.com/the-neoconservative-persuasion/article/4246.

Kristol, William. "Knowing What We Know Now, We Were Right To Fight In Iraq." *Media Matters*, 21 May 2015, mediamatters.org/blog/2015/05/21/iraq-war-architect-bill-kristol-knowing-what-we/203725.

Kristol, William and Robert Kagan. "Toward a Neo-Reaganite Foreign Policy." Reprinted from *Foreign Affairs*, July/Aug. 1996, *Carnegie Endowment for International Peace*, 1 July 1996, carnegieendowment.org/1996/07/01/toward-neo-reaganite-foreign-policy-pub-276.

La Ganga, Maria l. "Pop Quizzes Aside, Bush Continues Serious Study." *Los Angeles Times,* 19 Nov. 1999, articles.latimes.com/1999/nov/19/news/mn-35311.

Lancaster, John and Terry M. Neal. "Heavyweight 'Vulcans' Help Bush Forge a New Foreign Policy." *Washington Post,* 19 Nov. 1999, www.washingtonpost.com/archive/politics/199 9/11/19/heavyweight-vulcans-help-bush-forge-a-foreign-policy/015ae1fc-94ce-451b-944c-8f00ba906e8d/?utm_term=.a37649fe551f.

Ledeen, Michael A. "Scowcroft Strikes Out. A Familiar Cry." *National Review,* 6 Aug. 2002, web.archive.org/web/20090915185150/http://www.nationalreview.com/ledeen/ledeen080602a.asp. Accessed May 2017.

Lemann, Nicholas, "The Republicans: A Government Waits in Wings." *Washington Post,* 27 May 1980, www.washingtonpost.com/archive/politics/198 0/05/27/the-republicans-a-government-waits-in-wings/ae6f27a0-2269-48de-ad66-8e6ae6b88d33/?utm_term=.af7e7b27a040.

Leopold, Jason. "CIA Probe Finds Secret Pentagon Group Manipulated Intelligence on Iraqi Threat." *Dissident Voice*, 24 July 2003, dissidentvoice.org/Articles7/Leopold_OSP-Manipulation.htm.

Lewis, Charles and Mark Reading-Smith. "False Pretenses." *The Center for Public Integrity*, 23 Jan. 2008, www.publicintegrity.org/2008/01/23/5641/false-pretenses.

Linker, Damon. "The Philosopher and Everyone Else." *New Republic*, 30 July 2006, newrepublic.com/article/62904/the-philosopher-and-everyone else.

"List of Think Tanks in the United States." *Wikipedia*, last updated 19 Feb. 2019, en.wikipedia.org/wiki/List_of_think_tanks_in_the_United_States.

Lobe, Jim. "All in the Neocon Family." *AlterNet*, 26 Mar. 2003, www.alternet.org/story/15481/all_in_the_neocon_family.

---. "The Andean Condor Among the Hawks." *Asia Times Online*, Aug. 2003, www.atimes.com/atimes/Front_Page/EH15Aa01 .html.

---. "Leo Strauss' Philosophy of Deception." *AlterNet*, 18 May 2003, www.alternet.org/story/15935/leo_strauss%27_ philosophy__deception.

---. "Neoconservatism in a Nutshell." *Lobelog*, 24 Mar. 2016, lobelog.com/neoconservativism-in-a-nutshell/.

McGann, James. "The Think Tank Index." Reprinted from *Foreign Policy*, no. 170, Jan./Feb. 2009, *Wilson Web*, eclass.unipi.gr/modules/document/file.php/EB I115/The%20Think%20Tank%20Index.pdf.

Marusek, Sarah and David Miller. "The Brothers Who Funded Blair, Israeli Settlements and Islamophobia." *Middle East Eye*, 13 Aug. 2015, www.middleeasteye.net/columns/shared-funding-tony-blair-israeli-settlements-and-islamophobes-612558816.

Mason, Rowena, et al. "Tony Blair: 'I express more sorrow, regret and apology than you can ever believe.'" *The Guardian*, 6 July 2016,

www.theguardian.com/uk-
news/2016/jul/06/tony-blair-deliberately-
exaggerated-threat-from-iraq-chilcot-report-war-
inquiry.

Massing, Michael. "Now They Tell Us." *The New
York Review Books,* 26 Feb. 2004,
www.nybooks.com/articles/2004/02/26/now-
they-tell-us/.

Mayer, Jane. "The Manipulator: Ahmad Chalabi
pushed a tainted case for war. Can he survive
the occupation?" *The New Yorker,* 7 June 2004,
www.newyorker.com/magazine/2004/06/07/th
e-manipulator.

Mellon, Jerome. Review of *Silent Warfare:
Understanding the World of Intelligence,* 3rd ed.,
by Abram N. Shulsky and Gary J. Schmitt.
Journal of Conflict Studies, vol. 23, no. 2, Fall
2003,
journals.lib.unb.ca/index.php/JCS/article/view
/228/456.

Meyer, Dick. "Bush: The Decider-In-Chief." *CBS
News,* 20 April 2006,
www.cbsnews.com/news/bush-the-decider-in-
chief/.

Milstein, Mark. H. "Strategic Ties of Tentacles? Institute for National Security Affairs." *Washington Report on Middle East Affairs*, Oct. 1991, www.washingtonreport.me/1991-october/strategic-ties-or-tentacles-institute-for-national-security-affairs.html.

"Mission & History." *The Washington Institute for Near East Policy*, www.washingtoninstitute.org/about/mission-and-history.

Moore, James C. "Not Fit to Print." *Salon*, 27 May 2004, www.salon.com/2004/05/27/times_10/.

Morris, Roger. "The Road the U.S. Traveled to Baghdad Was Paved by 'Scoop' Jackson." Seattle *Post-Intelligencer*, 5 April 2003, www.seattlepi.com/news/article/P-I-Focus-The-road-the-U-S-traveled-to-Baghdad-1111242.php.

Mullin, Gemma. "Chilcot Report—What Were the Iraq Inquiry's Findings and ...?" *The Sun*, 6 July 2017 [anniversary date], www.thesun.co.uk/news/3957850/chilcot-report-iraq-inquiry-findings-tony-blair/.

Muravchik, Joshua. "The Future Is Neocon." *The National Interest*, 1 Sept. 2008, nationalinterest.org/greatdebate/neocons-realists/future-neocon-3803.

Murphy, Dan. "Iraq War: Predictions Made, and Results." *Christian Science Monitor*, 22 Dec. 2011, www.csmonitor.com/World/Backchannels/2011/1222/Iraq-war-Predictions-made-and-results.

"Neocon 101: What do Neoconservatives Believe?" *Christian Science Monitor*, 7 Aug. 2007, www.defenddemocracy.press/neocon-101-what-do-neoconservatives-believe/.

Newport, Frank. "Americans Still Think Iraq Had Weapons of Mass Destruction Before War." *Gallup*, 16 June 2003, www.gallup.com/poll/8623/americans-still-think-iraq-had-weapons-mass-destruction-before-war.aspx.

"1992 Draft Defense Planning Guidance." *Right Web*, 12 March 2008, rightweb.irc-online.org/profile/1992_Draft_Defense_Planning_Guidance/.

"Office of Special Plans." *Right Web*, 24 April 2011, rightweb.irc-online.org/profile/office_of_special_plans/.

Oldham, Kit. "Jackson, Henry M. 'Scoop' (1912–1983)." *HistoryLink.org Essay 5516*, 19 Aug. 2003, www.historylink.org/File/5516.

"Overview." *Obsession: Radical Islam's War Against the West*, www.precaution.ch/pdf/Obsession-Detailed_Overview_V1.1.pdf.

Pace, Eric. "Albert Wohlstetter, 83, Expert on U.S. Nuclear Strategy, Dies." *New York Times*, 14 Jan. 1997, www.nytimes.com/1997/01/14/world/albert-wohlstetter-83-expert-on-us-nuclear-strategy-dies.html.

"Peace in Israel and Palestine—What's Iraq got to do with It?" *SouthBay JVP*, 27 Feb. 2003, web.stanford.edu/group/peace/docs/march5th/BeninSanJose.doc.

Perle, Richard. "War Behind Closed Doors." *Frontline*, 25 Jan. 2003, www.pbs.org/wgbh/pages/frontline/shows/iraq/interviews/perle.html.

Pipes. Daniel. "Biography of Daniel Pipes." *Middle East Forum*, www.meforum.org/staff/Daniel+Pipes.

---. "Islamists—Not Who They Say They Are." *Jerusalem Post*, 9 May 2001, www.danielpipes.org/378/islamists-not-who-they-say-they-are.

---. "Japanese Internment: Why It Was a Good Idea—And the Lessons It Offers Today." *HNN History News Network*, 10 Jan. 2005, historynewsnetwork.org/article/9289.

---. "The Middle East Forum." *Daniel Pipes Middle East Forum*, www.danielpipes.org/mef.php.

---. "The Muslims Are Coming! The Muslims Are Coming!" *Daniel Pipes Middle East Forum*, original text submitted to *National Review*, published 19 Nov. 1990, www.danielpipes.org/198/the-muslims-are-coming-the-muslims-are-coming.

---. "WE NEED MUSLIM INTERNMENT CAMPS NOW*!!!*" *Middle East Forum*, 20 June 2006, www.danielpipes.org/comments/47920.

---. "Who is the Enemy?" *Commentary*, Jan. 2002, www.danielpipes.org/103/who-is-the-enemy.

Pipes, Daniel and Christopher C. Hull. "A White House Initiative to Defeat Radical Islam." *Washington Times*, 20 Feb. 2017, www.danielpipes.org/17280/white-house-initiative-defeat-radical-islam.

Podhoretz, Norman. "Now, Instant Zionism." *New York Times*, 3 Feb. 1974, www.nytimes.com/books/99/02/21/specials/podhoretz-zion.html.

Postel, Danny. "Noble Lies and Perpetual War: Leo Strauss, the Neocons, and Iraq." *openDemocracy*, 16 Oct. 2003, www.opendemocracy.net/en/article_1542jsp/.

"President Bill Clinton's State of the Union Address [text]." *AllPolitics*, January 27, 1998, www.cnn.com/ALLPOLITICS/1998/01/27/sotu/transcripts/clinton/.

"Presidential Power-The Bush Legacy (Cheney's Law)." PBS *Frontline*, 16 Oct. 2007, www.pbs.org/wgbh//pages/frontline/cheney/themes/cheneyview.html.

"Profile: Lewis 'Scooter' Libby." *BBC News*, 3 July 2007, news.bbc.co.uk/2/hi/americas/4353710.stm.

"Promoting American Interests." *Middle East Forum*, 22 Mar. 2017, powerbase.info/index.php/Middle_East_Forum.

Reeve, Elspeth. "Team Iraqi Freedom: Where Are They Now?" *The Atlantic*, 19 Mar. 2013, www.theatlantic.com/politics/archive/2013/03/bush-administration-iraq-where-are-they-now/317216/.

Reuter, Tim. "Donald Rumsfeld's Maddening Confession in the Unknown Known." *Forbes Contributors*, 14 May 2005, www.forbes.com/sites/timreuter/2014/05/05/donald-rumsfelds-maddening-confession-in-the-unknown-known/#7649ecab5a0e.

"Richard Perle-biography," *JewAge*, www.jewage.org/wiki/en/Profile:P1236851091.

"Robert Kagan." *Right Web*, 7 Sept. 2016, rightweb.irc-online.org/profile/kagan_robert/.

Rosenau, Josh. "Research Methodology101." *ScienceBlogs*, 12 Dec. 2011, scienceblogs.com/tfk/2011/12/12/research-methodology-101/.

Rozenberg, Joshua. "The Iraq War Inquiry Has Left the Door Open for Tony Blair to Be Prosecuted." *The Guardian*, 7 May 2017, www.theguardian.com/commentisfree/2016/jul/06/iraq-war-inquiry-chilcot-tony-blair-prosecute.

Sanders, Richard. "What Did Happen To Saddam's WMD?" *History Today*, 12 July 2016, www.historytoday.com/richard-sanders/what-did-happen-saddam%E2%80%99s-wmd.

Schmitt, Eric. "Threats and Responses: Military Spending; Pentagon Contradicts General on Iraq Occupation Force's Size." *New York Times*, 28 Feb.2003, www.nytimes.com/2003/02/28/us/threats-responses-military-spending-pentagon-contradicts-general-iraq-occupation.html.

"Scooter-Biography." *JewAge*, www.jewage.org/wiki/en/Article:Scooter_Libby_–_Biography.

Shatz, Adam. "The Native Informant." *The Nation, 10 April 2003,* www.thenation.com/article/native-informant/.

---. "Short Cuts." *London Review of Books,* 9 Oct. 2008, www.lrb.co.uk/v30/n19/adam-shatz/short-cuts.

Shavit, Ari. "White Man's Burden." *Haaretz,* 3 April 2003, www.haaretz.com/israel-news/white-man-s-burden-1.14110.

St. Clair, Jeffrey. "War Pimps." *Counterpunch,* 14 Aug. 2003, www.counterpunch.org/2003/08/14/war-pimps/.

Steele, Jonathan. "Ahmed Chalabi Obituary." *The Guardian,* 4 Nov. 2015, www.theguardian.com/world/2015/nov/04/ahmed-chalabi.

Stern, Jessica. "The Invasion of Iraq Was an Engine of Terrorist Growth." *US News,* 20 Mar. 2013, www.usnews.com/debate-club/10-years-later-was-the-iraq-war-worth-it/the-invasion-of-iraq-was-an-engine-of-terrorist-growth.

Stolberg, Sheryl Gay. "Bush Spares Libby 30-Month Jail Term." *New York Times*, 2 July 2007, www.nytimes.com/2007/07/02/washington/02 cnd-libby.html.

Suellentrop, Chris. "Richard Perle: Washington's Faceful Bureaucrat." *Slate*, 23 Aug. 2002, www.slate.com/articles/news_and_politics/asse ssment/2002/08/richard_perle.html.

Swidey, Neil. "Strategy Guru Albert Wohlstetter Spent Decades Arguing for Military Flexibility and Precision Targeting. But Have His Washington Disciples Learned His Real Lessons?" *boston.com News*, 18 May 2003, archive.boston.com/news/globe/ideas/articles/ 2003/05/18/the_analyst/?page=2. *The Boston Globe*, The Mind of the Administration—Part Two: The Analyst.

Thielmann, Greg. "Interview—Truth, War Consequences." *Frontline*, 9 Oct. 2003, www.pbs.org/wgbh/pages/frontline/shows/trut h/interviews/thielmann.html.

"Timeline: The Life & Times of Donald Rumsfeld." *Frontline*, 26 Oct. 2004, www.pbs.org/wgbh/pages/frontline/shows/pen tagon/etc/cronfeld.html.

Timm, Trevor. "The US Needs Its Own Chilcot Report." *The Guardian*, 6 July 2016, www.theguardian.com/commentisfree/2016/jul/06/us-george-bush-needs-chilcot-report-iraq-war.

"Top 10 Bush Figures We'll Miss [John Bolton]." *Time*, Jan. 2016, content.time.com/time/specials/packages/article/0,28804,1872508_1872490_1872488,00.html.

Trotta, Daniel. "Iraq War Costs U.S. More Than $2 Trillion: Study." *Reuters*, 14 Mar. 2013, www.reuters.com/article/us-iraq-war-anniversary/iraq-war-costs-u-s-more-than-2-trillion-study-idUSBRE92D0PG20130314.

Tyler, Patrick E. "U.S. Strategy Plan Calls for Insuring No Rivals Develop." *New York Times*, 3 Mar. 1992, www.nytimes.com/1992/03/08/world/us-strategy-plan-calls-for-insuring-no-rivals-develop.html?pagewanted=1.

Unger, Craig. "How Cheney Took Control of Bush's Foreign Policy." *Salon*, 9 Nov. 2007, www.salon.com/2007/11/09/house_of_bush_3/.

University of Washington Research Guides.
"Senator Henry M. Jackson, 1912–1983: Staff."
University Libraries, 22 Feb. 2018,
guides.lib.uw.edu/research/henry_jackson/staff

Vergano, Dan. "Half-Million Iraqis Died in the
War, New Study Says." *National Geographic*, 16
Oct. 2013,
news.nationalgeographic.com/news/2013/10/1
31015-iraq-war-deaths-survey-2013/.

Verlöy, André and Daniel Politi. "Advisors of
Influence: Nine Members of the Defense Policy
Board Have Ties to Defense Contractors." *Center
for Public Integrity*, 28 Mar. 2003,
www.publicintegrity.org/2003/03/28/3157/adv
isors-influence-nine-members-defense-policy-
board-have-ties-defense-contractors.

Vest, Jason. "The Men From JINSA and CSP."
The Nation, 15 Aug. 2002,
www.thenation.com/article/men-jinsa-and-
csp/.

Vogler, Gary. "The Truth about Oil and the Iraq
War, 15 Years Later." *University Press of Kansas
Blog*, 24 April 2018,
universitypressblog.dept.ku.edu/uncategorized/
1395/.

Walsh, John. "Lies of the Neocons: From Leo Strauss to Scooter Libby." *OpEdNews.com*, 9 Nov. 2005, www.opednews.com/articles/opedne_john_wal_051109_lies_of_the_neocons_.htm.

Ward, Nathaniel. "Victor Davis Hanson vs. Ronald Edsforth: The Iraq War." *Dartmouth Review*, 11 Feb.2005, historynewsnetwork.org/article/10322.

Watson Institute, Brown University. "US & Allied Killed and Wounded." *Costs of War*, April 2015, watson.brown.edu/costsofwar/costs/human/military.

Wattenberg, Ben. "Richard Perle: The Making of a Neoconservative." *Think Tank*, 14 Nov. 2002, www.pbs.org/thinktank/transcript1017.html.

Whitaker, Brian. "Bush's Historian." *The Guardian*, 2 May 2006, www.theguardian.com/commentisfree/2006/may/02/thehistoryman.

---. "Selective Memri." *The Guardian*, 12 Aug. 2002, www.theguardian.com/world/2002/aug/12/worlddispatch.brianwhitaker.

---. "US Thinktanks Give Lessons in Foreign Policy." *The Guardian*, 19 Aug. 2002, www.theguardian.com/world/2002/aug/19/wor lddispatch.

Winans, James A. "A Speech Is Not Merely an Essay Standing on Its Hind Legs." 1931. *Joyful Public Speaking (from fear to Joy)*, 28 Jan. 2014, joyfulpublicspeaking.blogspot.com/2014/01/a-speech-is-not-same-as-essay.

Wohlstetter, Albert. "The Delicate Balance of Terror." *Rand Corporation*, p. 1472, 6 November 1958, rev. December 1958, www.rand.org/about/history/wohlstetter/P1472/P1472.html.

"Woolsey, R. James." *Right Web*, 5 Jan. 2017, rightweb.irconline.org/profile/woolsey_james/.

---. "World War IV." *Free Republic*, 21 Nov. 2002, www.freerepublic.com/focus/news/794129/pos ts.

Zeller, Tom. "Father Strauss Knows Best." *Harpers*, 4 May 2003, www.nytimes.com/2003/05/04/weekinreview/t he-nation-father-strauss-knows-best.html.

Appendix

In 2009, given political and public pressure at the end of UK participation in the war, Prime Minister Gordon Brown launched the inquiry of his country's role in the 2003 invasion of Iraq. Seventy-one-year-old Sir John Chilcot, Cambridge graduate and honored civil servant, was named to head the investigating committee of four: three more knights and a baroness.

Completion of the Chilcot report was announced in July of 2016, years after the anticipated completion date. One reason for the long delay related to difficulties in accomplishing declassification of documents, e.g., communications between Prime Minister Tony Blair and President George W. Bush.

Public interest in Britain was high, and the Chilcot group strove to make their important publication universally available. It was placed in libraries and other public places. The press printed summaries, typically brief accounts of 1,000 to 1,200 words, such as an annotated listing of a dozen or so prime conclusions. Websites were set up to disseminate pertinent information and copies of the report. An "Executive Summary" of 150 pages was—and is—readily accessible for review and copying. Aware of high public interest, the Chilcot group was resolved to demonstrate openness.

The Guardian published a summary immediately on July 6, 2016, announcing, "The Chilcot inquiry has delivered a damning verdict on the decision by former prime minister Tony Blair to commit British troops to the US-led invasion of Iraq in 2003." They selected fourteen principal points in censure and quoted from the report:

The UK chose to join the invasion before peaceful options had been exhausted

Chilcot is withering about Blair's choice to join the US invasion. He says: "We have concluded that the UK chose to join the invasion of Iraq before the peaceful options for disarmament had been exhausted. Military action at that time was not a last resort."

Blair deliberately exaggerated the threat posed by Saddam Hussein

Chilcot finds that Blair deliberately exaggerated the threat posed by the Iraqi regime as he sought to make the case for military action to MPs and the public in the buildup to the invasion in 2002 and 2003.

The then prime minister disregarded warnings about the potential consequences of military action, and relied too heavily on his own beliefs, rather than the more nuanced judgments of the intelligence services. "The judgments about Iraq's capabilities ... were presented with a certainty that was not justified," the report says.

Blair promised George Bush: 'I will be with you, whatever'

Tony Blair wrote to George W Bush eight months before the Iraq invasion to offer his unqualified backing for war well before UN weapons inspectors had completed their work, saying: "I will be with you, whatever." In a six-page memo marked secret and personal, the then British prime minister told Bush, US president at the time, in July 2002 that the removal of Saddam Hussein would "free up the region" even if Iraqis may "feel ambivalent about being invaded". It was one of 29 letters Blair sent to Bush in the run-up to the Iraq war, during the conflict and in its devastating aftermath, released on Wednesday as part of the Chilcot report.

The decision to invade was made in unsatisfactory circumstances

Chilcot finds that the decision made by Tony Blair's cabinet's [sic] to invade was made in circumstances that were "far from satisfactory". The inquiry did not reach a view on the legality of the war, saying this could only be assessed by a "properly constituted and internationally recognised court", but did make a damning assessment of how the decision was made. The process for deciding that the war was legal is described as "perfunctory" by the inquiry, while "no formal record was made of that decision, and the precise grounds on which it was made remains unclear".

George Bush largely ignored UK advice on postwar planning

The inquiry found that the Bush administration repeatedly over-rode advice from the UK on how to oversee Iraq after the invasion, including the involvement of the United Nations, the control of Iraqi oil money and the extent to which better security should be put at the heart of the military operation. The inquiry specifically criticises the way in which the US dismantled the security apparatus of the Saddam Hussein army and describes the whole invasion as a strategic failure.

There was no imminent threat from Saddam

Iran, North Korea and Libya were considered greater threats in terms of nuclear, chemical and biological weapons proliferation, and the UK joint intelligence committee believed it would take Iraq five years, after the lifting of sanctions, to produce enough fissile material for a weapon, Chilcot finds. Britain's previous strategy of containment could have been adopted and continued for some time.

Britain's intelligence agencies produced 'flawed information'

The Chilcot report identifies a series of major blunders by the British intelligence services that produced "flawed" information about Saddam's alleged weapons of mass destruction, the basis for going to war. Chilcot says the intelligence community worked from the start on the misguided assumption that Saddam had WMDs and made no attempt to consider the possibility that he had got rid of them, which he had.

The UK military were ill-equipped for the task

The UK's military involvement in Iraq ended with the "humiliating" decision to strike deals with enemy militias because British forces were seriously ill-equipped and there was "wholly inadequate" planning and preparation for life after Saddam Hussein, the Chilcot report finds. The Ministry of

*Defence (MoD) planned the invasion in a
rush and was slow to react to the security
threats on the ground, particularly the use
of improvised explosive devices (IEDs) that
killed so many troops, the report says.*

UK-US relations would not have been harmed if UK stayed out of war

*Chilcot rejects the view that the UK would
have lost diplomatic influence if it had
refused to join the war. "Blair was right to
weigh the possible consequences for the
wider alliance with the US very carefully,"
the report says. But it adds: "If the UK had
refused to join the US in the war it would
not have led to a fundamental or lasting
change in the UK's relationship with the
US."*

Blair ignored warnings on what would happen in Iraq after invasion

*The report says that between early 2002
and March 2003 Blair was told that, post-
invasion, Iraq could degenerate into civil
war. In September 2002, the US secretary
of state, Colin Powell, predicted "a terrible*

*bloodletting of revenge after Saddam goes",
adding: "Traditional in Iraq after conflict."
Sir Christopher Meyer, UK ambassador to
the US, added: "It will probably make
pacifying Afghanistan look like child's
play." Chilcot rejects Blair's claim that the
subsequent chaos and sectarian conflict
could not have been predicted.*

The government had no post-invasion strategy

*According to Chilcot, Blair did not identify
which ministers were responsible for
postwar planning and strategy. The prime
minister also failed to press Bush for
"definitive assurances" about the US's
post-conflict plans. Nor did he envisage
anything other than the best-case scenario
once the invasion was over: that a US-led
and UN-authorised force would find itself
operating in a "relatively benign security
environment". All of this contributed to
Britain's ultimate strategic failure.*

The UK had no influence on Iraq's postwar US-run administration

The Bush administration appointed ambassador Paul Bremer to head a new coalition provisional authority in Baghdad. The UK had practically no input into subsequent decisions taken by Bremer, including the dissolving of Saddam's army and security structures. This decision alienated the Sunni community and fed the insurgency. Blair continued to talk to Bush, but Britain had little influence on the ground over day-to-day policymaking.

The UK did not achieve its objectives in Iraq

Chilcot says that by 2009, when UK forces were pulled out of Iraq, Downing Street was facing strategic failure. Iraq was gripped by "deep sectarian divisions". There was a fragile situation in Basra, rows over oil revenues, and rampant corruption inside Iraqi government ministries. No evidence had been found that Saddam had weapons of mass destruction. During this period the government did not reappraise the situation, Chilcot says. He describes as "meagre" the results of Britain's costly six-year occupation.

The government did not try hard enough to keep a tally of Iraqi civilian casualties

Before the war, Blair had said that the US-led invasion coalition would try to minimise civilian casualties. As the war and occupation unfolded, however, the MoD made only a "broad estimate" of how many Iraqis were being killed. The report says that more time was devoted to which department should have responsibility for the issue than was spent on finding out the number. The government's main interest was to "rebut accusations that coalition forces were responsible for the deaths of large numbers" of Iraqis. (Chilcot Reports)

US-UK Comparison: A Moot Matter

After publication of the Chilcot report, all major UK newspapers put blame for the Iraq tragedy squarely onto Prime Minister Tony Blair.

Absent an inquiry into all critical aspects of the invasion of Iraq, the needy people of the US have been left "adrift," one might say. They have not been offered the benefits of national introspection, wrenching though that therapy would be.

Moreover, without a thorough US investigation, this study cannot contrast press or public reactions in the two countries. Authoritative judgment in the US remains suspended.

We do know that, in the US, all major dailies supported the invasion. In the UK, *The Guardian, Mirror,* and *Daily Mail* argued against attacking Iraq. All of Rupert Murdoch's newspapers favored the invasion: the *Times, Sun,* and *Sunday Times.*

The London *Sun,* a tabloid favoring the war, reported on the results rather plainly, finding that Britain's prime minister "rushed into war prematurely":

- "Military action was not a last resort, and the UK chose to join the invasion of Iraq before all peaceful options for disarmament had been exhausted.

- There was no imminent threat from Saddam Hussein in March 2003 and intelligence had 'not established beyond doubt' that he had continued to produce chemical weapons.

- Tony Blair assured US President George W Bush 'I will be with you whatever,' in a memo eight months before the war.

- [There was a] catastrophic failure to plan properly for both the war and keeping the peace after it, leading swiftly to pandemonium on southern Iraq's streets as well as serious equipment shortfalls for British troops—179 of who were killed.

- Blair discarded repeated and major warnings inside government about how the invasion could hike the terrorist threat and about 'the magnitude' of the task in rebuilding Iraq after Saddam's toppling.

- There were major intelligence failings by senior spies, headed up by Joint Intelligence Committee boss and later MI6 chief Sir John Scarlett, and their assessments should have been challenged.

- The decisions to proceed with military action from a legal perspective were 'far from satisfactory' with the thinking behind Attorney General Lord Goldsmith's final green light for it 'not clear'.

- There was 'little time' to prepare troops properly for deployment in Iraq and the risks were neither 'properly identified' and resulted in 'equipment shortfalls'.

- UK forces faced gaps in some key capability areas including armoured tanks, reconnaissance and intelligence assets - and it's not clear who was responsible for identifying such issues." (Mullin)

Editors of *The Times* of London, owned by Rupert Murdoch, followed publication of the Chilcot numerically.

The Chilcot report by numbers:

- "2.6m words in the Chilcot report. That makes it 4½ times bigger than War and Peace (587,000 words) and about 3 times bigger than the Bible (775,000) and the complete works of Shakespeare (885,000).

- £767 to buy all 12 volumes of Sir John's report

- £30 for the 15-page executive summary

- 7 years since the inquiry was launched

- 2,578 days have passed since report was announced by Gordon Brown

- 179 British forces have died in Iraq

- 150,000 government documents scrutinised

"If all that doesn't sound like enough reading, there are several books about the war, including:

- *The Assassins' Gate: America in Iraq* by George Packer, which was among the three finalists for the Pulitzer prize in the general non-fiction category in 2006 [pro invasion]

- *Fiasco: The American Military....*" ("The Chilcot Report by Numbers")

"Return to Greatness"

Few would argue with the basic American belief that insufficient public access to information on political activity hampers the functioning of democracy. When relevant data on vital issues are arbitrarily concealed, the people's participation and assistance necessarily are curbed. As the Supreme Court declared in 1936, "An informed public is the most potent of all restraints upon misgovernment" (*Grosjean* 250). Such a comment seems trite now but remains an ideal, nonetheless.

The people did not know that the US government had definitely developed a plan to invade Iraq. Left out and frustrated in sensing existence of covert activity, they marched by the millions in street parades, but the US government was unresponsive. Though expected to be a central part—for many, a life-threating part—of the eventual operation, the people were not consulted on meaningful issues: need, right and wrong, legality, adequacy of planning related to execution, etc. No official debate was sanctioned on essential questions. Serious consultation with well-known cultural anthropologists who know of Iraqi values and behavioral predispositions would have helped to prevent mistakes in decision making. Secretary Rumsfeld was mistaken on major questions regarding logistical matters. Reliable and noncommitted experts on Middle Eastern political structures were available for counsel. The entire enterprise was hurried and carried off without use of important resources. Remember Justice Louis Brandeis's (*trite,* again) democratic statement of value: "Sunlight is said to be the best of disinfectants"?

Costs of indifference and ignorance in cultural, political, logistical, and religious concerns were phenomenal.

One studying the history of the time envisions a hurry-up, pell-mell venture. When our system of government is made to work right, it encourages—and patiently tolerates—great care, debate, free choice, consultation, and transparency.

Thus, The Recommendation

May the current patriotic servants of the United States in their wisdom and valor now choose a course of health for a weakened nation, and may responsible leaders establish a process allowing for a cleansing of the national soul. The people must come to face and deal with details of the wrongdoing.

Index

Abrams, Elliott, 30–33,
  158
  bellicosity, 32
  Henry M. Jackson
    and, 15, 30, 179
  JINSA and, 69
  PNAC and, 122, 123
  rhetor, 168
  under Ronald
    Reagan, 30, 113
  Woolsey and, 57
Addington, David S.,
  57, 159
Adelman, Kenneth, 57,
  185
administrative triad,
  213, *See also* White
  House, *See also*
  Bush-Cheney-
  Rumsfeld nationalist
  triad, function of
AEI. *See* American
  Enterprise Institute
al-Haideri, Adnan
  Ihsan Saeed, 89
al-Janabi, Rafid
  Ahmed Alwan
  ("Curveball"), 78

al-Qaeda, 95, 98, 111,
  164, 165, 175–77,
  178, 197
American Enterprise
  Institute (AEI)
  Bush address at,
    65–67
  members, 38, 46,
    47, 66, 105
  Michael Ledeen and,
    106
  origin and activities,
    65–67
Armitage, Richard L.,
  123, 124, 130, 137
axis of evil, 177
Baker, Jim, 6, 37
Bell, Daniel, 17
Benador, Eleana /
  Benador Associates,
  84–87
Bennett, William J.,
  102, 122, 124
bin Laden, Osama, 28,
  109
Blair, Tony, and
  Chilcot report, 207,
  272–74, 277–80

George W. Bush
and, 271, 273–
75, 277–79, 282
UK media on, 280–
83
Bolton, John, 35–38,
66, 124
as undersecretary of
state for Arms
Control and
International
Security, 36, 158
David Wurmser and,
46
JINSA and, 69
MEMRI advisory
board member,
71
Boot, Max, 57, 85
Breindel, Eric, 58, 114
Brookings Institution,
74, 96
Brooks, David, 93–94
and uses of rhetoric,
91, 93
rhetorical appeal of
vs. James
Woolsey's appeal,
52

writer for the
Weekly Standard,
93
Bryen, Stephen, 57,
68, 69
Bunker, of Henry M.
Jackson, 14, 15, 24,
179
Bush, G.H.W.
and Iran-Contra
pardon of
Abrams, 33
and Perle's
membership of
Defense Policy
Advisory Board,
24
association with Jim
Baker and Brent
Scowcroft, 6
Bolton under, 36
Cheney under, 116,
140
father of George W.
Bush, 127, 129
Wolfowitz with, 20
Woolsey under, 50
Bush, George W., 127–
32, 213
and relationship
with Cheney, 65,

140, 144, 145,
150, 214
appointments, 24,
36–37, 40, 158,
279
as the "decider",
137–39, 199, 213
Chilcot report on,
271, 273–74,
275, 278, 279,
282
development in
military presence,
176
grooming to meet
deficiencies, 3,
115, 130, 135,
143
interpersonal
competence of,
136
repeated lying and
false assumptions
of, 179, 197, 203
son of G.H.W. Bush,
3, 48
speech delivery of,
175–77, 197–99
speeches

bullhorn speech
(September 14,
2001), 136
inaugural
(January 29,
2001), 133,
135
on deck of aircraft
carrier (May 1,
2003), 202
September 11
address to the
nation, 164
September 20
address to
Congress, 176
State of the Union
of 2002, 177
ultimatum to
Iraq, 194–97
Tony Blair and,
271–75, 277–79,
282
Bush-Cheney-
Rumsfeld nationalist
triad, function of, 4,
175, 200, *See also*
administrative triad,
See also White
House

Carnegie Endowment for International Peace, 74, 96
Carter, Jimmy, 20, 50
Chalabi, Ahmed, 75–78, 183–84
  Albert J. Wohlstetter and, 75
  Cheney and, 76, 146
  David Wurmser and, 47
  Iraqi National Congress and, 75, 86, 183
  Judith Miller and, 79
  OSP and, 184
  Rendon Group and, 88, 89, 90
  selling of regime change in Iraq, 76, 78, 82
  Wolfowitz and, 76
Cheney, Richard B., 17, 139–43, 145, 214
  as Bush's running mate, 3, 115, 132
  association with intellectuals, 146–48
  David Addington as legal counsel for, 159
  David Armstrong's essay on, 152
  delegation with Bush and, 3, 143, 144
  Donald Rumsfeld and, 3, 146, 158, 176
  draft deferments, 142, 149
  elements of a neoconservative, 152–57, 195
  JINSA and, 69
  John Bolton and, 37
  nationalist hawk, 43, 116, 118
  nationalistic leadership, 144
  notable political savvy, 3, 143–46
  OSP and, 179
  PNAC and, 122
  pragmatism of, 146
  Rumsfeld and, 162

Scooter Libby and,
39, 40, 115, 145,
158
suasory, 3, 130,
142, 151
VFW speech, 156,
149–57, 197
Wolfowitz and, 21,
115
Chilcot report
as a useful model,
211
George W. Bush, on,
271–75, 278–79
Guardian summary,
271–80
media reactions to,
280–84
Sir John Chilcot, as
author of, 206,
271
Churchill, Winston,
53, 55
*Clean Break–A New
Strategy for Securing
the Realm, A*, 46,
71, 119–20
Clinton, William, 24,
50, 104, 115, 123–
25, 140
CNN, 27, 28

Cohen, Eliot A., 57,
122
cohesion. *See also*
consubstantiality
as decisive element
of
neoconservative
persuasion, 4,
188–93, 199, 200
rhetoric and, 57,
199–200
unity in
identification,
188, 199
White House, 4, 199
Cold War, 5, 12, 48,
49, 56, 117, 147,
154, 166
Commentary magazine,
17, 31, 108, 187
communism/communi
st(s), 5, 15, 45
consubstantiality. *See
also* cohesion
and cohesion, Irving
Kristol and, 191
and togetherness,
188–93
as measure of
success in
rhetorical

interaction, 188–
93, 214
Barrett and, 189
Burke and (neocons
"acting upon
themselves"), 189
neocon success in
cohesion and,
188–93
containment, 6, 7,
154, 173, 276
Decter, Midge, 58, 122
Defense Planning
Guidance (DPG),
1992, 39, 115, 116–
18
Defense Policy
Advisory Board
Committee, 24–27,
39, 51, 158, 190
"Delicate Balance of
Terror" paper
(Wohlstetter), 23
democracy, 2, 7, 21,
56, 77, 78, 93, 210,
284
Department of Defense
(DoD), 15, 19, 20,
21, 34, 38, 62, 105,
116, 158, 159, 180,
189, 190

Dobriansky, Paula, 57,
122, 124
DoD. *See* Department
of Defense
DPG. *See* Defense
Planning Guidance
(DPG)
Drury, Shadia B., 8, 9
educational
institutions,
universities and
colleges
Harvard, 1, 30, 33,
61, 62, 81, 94,
96, 102, 127
Johns Hopkins, 20,
46, 70
Naval War College,
62
Stanford, 33, 49
University of
Chicago, 1, 9, 11,
13, 19, 39, 62,
75, 93
University of
Pennsylvania, 62,
102
Yale, 1, 35, 38, 49,
96, 127, 139, 146
Encounter magazine,
18

Endowment for Middle East Truth (EMET), 71, 73–74

ethos, 91, 142, 150, 167, 174

eventful decades, 1980s and 1990s as, 113–15

evil, 1, 6, 9, 22, 55–56, 79, 94, 95, 155, 164, 170, 177, 194, 201, 202, 212, 213

Feith, Douglas, 15, 33–35, 47, 66, 69, 71, 76, 119, 146, 152, 158, 179, 182, 189–91, 200, 212

and security breaches, 35, 183

War and Decision book on Iraq intervention, 35

foreign policy of US, 2, 11, 30, 32, 51, 59, 85, 97, 98, 100, 104, 105, 113, 115, 119, 123, 129, 143, 145

realpolitik as. *See* realism

Friedberg, Aaron, 58, 122

Friedman, Tom, 91–93

Frontline, 27, 28, 97

Frum, David, 57, 66, 177

Fukuyama, Francis, 122, 124

Gaffney, Frank, 15, 57, 85, 122

Gerson, Michael

and "axis of evil" phrase, 177

as Bush's speechwriter, 132–35, 177

evangelical Christian, 132, 177

Guardian newspaper, 72, 272–80

Hanson, Victor Davis, writings of, 146–48

hawk(s), political, 12, 14, 22, 38, 39, 43, 51, 78, 85, 131, 191, 201

hegemony, advocacy of, 6–7, 55, 96, 97, 105, 121

Heritage Foundation,
31, 74
Hersh, Seymour, 27,
184, 192
Hudson Institute, 31,
69, 70, 71, 180
Hussein, Saddam, 92,
93, 194, 275, 276
claims against, 28,
42, 43, 45, 81,
82, 88, 98, 123,
124, 153, 181,
183, 184, 194,
197, 282
push for removal of,
2, 22, 46, 47, 51,
59, 78, 97, 103,
104, 115, 123,
155, 156, 165,
195, 273, 274
INC. *See* Iraqi National
Congress (INC)
Institute for Advanced
Strategic and
Political Studies
(IASPS), 46, 71
invasion of Iraq. *See
also* Iraq
lead-up to, 35, 40,
75, 86, 87, 90,
94, 98, 106–7,

132, 165, 178,
179, 181, 273,
281
false assertions of
ties to al-
Qaeda and
9/11, 28, 95,
98, 177, 184
false assertions of
WMDs and,
41–42, 66, 78,
79–80, 88, 89,
99, 104, 124–
25, 153, 154,
181, 195–97,
206, 275
JINSA and, 51
promotion by
neoconservativ
es, 2, 21, 83,
91, 146, 190,
193, 200
promotion by
White House
leadership, 4,
67, 149, 175–
77, 185, 193,
194, 200
push for regime
change in, 2,
22, 46, 49, 51,

76, 100, 103,
106, 126, 156,
170, 203
US newspapers'
complicity in,
81
Valerie Plame
scandal and,
45
predictions of easy
success in, 104,
156
subsequent to, 104,
160, 195, 277
Chilcot report,
206, 271–84
gradual reduction
in military
presence, 204
havoc and costs,
203–5, 211
lack of US report
on, 207–11,
281, 284–86
Iran, 37, 56, 106, 177,
275
Iran-Contra affair, 33,
105, 113
Iraq, 26, 47–49, 58–59,
70, 77, 159, 160,

See also invasion of
Iraq
Bush ultimatum
address to, 194–
97
end of Gulf War
and, 116
Feith book on
invasion of, 34
Woolsey's "World
War IV" and, 52,
56
Iraqi National
Congress (INC), 47,
76, 78, 86, 88, 183
Islamophobia, 72
Israel, 16, 32–33, 46,
76, 115, 119
John Bolton and, 38
Likud party of, 64,
67, 68, 71, 119,
183
MEMRI and, 72
OSP and, 183
Podhoretz on, 186
Rumsfeld and, 160
security of
Irving Kristol's
publications as
platform for
ideas on, 18

Libby's interest
in, 41
needs coupled
with US's, 2,
41, 47, 55, 63,
67, 68, 73,
109, 120
Strauss on, 10
Woolsey's support
of, aggressive
approach to,
51
Zionism and, 186–
87
Jackson, Henry M.,
14–16, 19, 23, 30,
33
Albert J. Wohlstetter
and, 14
as hawk, 14
Bunker of, 14, 15,
24, 179
JINSA service
award, 16, 69
migration of
Russian Jews
and, 16
on civil rights, 14,
51
supporter of
neocons and, 2,

7, 14, 131, 179,
190
Jewish identity
as Zionists, 186
entry to the Bunker
of young neocons
with, 14
faith and
spirituality, 32–
33
immigration of
Russians with, 16
neocon roots to, 132
question of unity,
58, 186
stance on war in
American, 58–59
Strauss and, 8
Jewish Institute for
National Security
Affairs (JINSA), 51,
67, 68, 106
origin and actions,
67–69
Senator Henry M.
"Scoop" Jackson
Distinguished
Service Award by,
winners of, 16, 69
JINSA. See Jewish
Institute for

National Security
Affairs
Kagan, Donald, 57, 70,
  122, 187
Kagan, Frederick, 57,
  66, 187
Kagan, Robert, 57, 96–
  102, 103, 121, 124,
  187, 191, 212
  advocate for
    "benevolent
    hegemony", 96,
    97, 105
  as prominent
    neocon, 57
  as rhetor—writer
    and speaker, 52,
    85, 96, 97–102,
    105, 114, 165–
    71, 173–74
  member of WINEP,
    64
Khalilzad, Zalmay, 15,
  39, 116, 118
PNAC, 122, 124
Kissinger, Henry, 27,
  70, 101, 154
Krauthammer,
  Charles, 85, 94–95,
  212

as rhetor, 52, 91,
  94, 114
Kristol, Irving, 17–18,
  102
  as founder of
    neoconservatism,
    2, 7, 17
  as supporter of
    neoconservative
    writing, 18
  founder of *National
    Interest* magazine,
    113
  neoconservatism as
    a persuasion, 17,
    192
  New Republic
    contributor, 114
  wife Gertrude
    Himmelfarb and,
    187
Kristol, William, 102–
  5, 124, 191
  advocacy of attack
    on Iraq, 104
  and PNAC, 96, 103,
    121
  and *The Weekly
    Standard*, 103,
    121
  as rhetor, 98–100

Robert Kagan, coauthor with, 96, 98–100, 102, 105

Wolfowitz and, 212

Ledeen, Michael, 66, 85, 105–7

as JINSA founding member and executive director, 68, 106

as rhetor, 52, 114, 170

Heilbrunn on, 107

Lewis, Bernard, 57, 71, 146

Libby, I. Lewis 'Scooter', 38–46, 122, 200

at center of government, 39, 145

awards, 41

Cheney and, 39, 115, 145, 146, 152, 158

conviction, 44

finesse as rhetor, 191

loyalty of questioned, 41

Valerie Plame scandal and, 42–46

with Khalilzad, as DPG coauthors, 39, 116–18

Wolfowitz and, 38–39, 116, 212

Lieberman, Joe, 16, 69

Likud, conservative party of Israel, 67, 68, 71, 119, 183

Lobe, Jim, 55–57, 191

logos, 91, 93

Los Angeles Times, 85, 108

Luti, William J., 76, 182

Massing, Michael, 80–81

MEF. See Middle East Forum

MEMRI. See Middle East Media Research Institute

Middle East, 2, 34, 41, 62, 75–76, 81, 285

claims of proliferation of WMDs in, 19, 66, 88

focus of publications
and think tanks
on, 46–49, 65,
70, 71–72, 85,
88, 89, 106, 119,
126, 147, 166
justification of force
to establish
democracy or
peace in, 7, 8,
106, 156
rhetoric on, 54, 56,
168–71
security of Israel
and America, 32,
63, 109, 119–21,
168–71
Middle East Forum
(MEF)
"Campus Watch", 63
Daniel Pipes as
leader and
principal
spokesperson for,
63, 107, 111
David Wurmser as
member of, 46
donations to and
from, 112
Eleana Benador
and, 85

origin and scope,
61, 62
Middle East Media
Research Institute
(MEMRI)
Meyrav Wurmser as
cofounder and
executive
director, 71
purpose and
accusations
against, 71–73
Miller, Judith, as
instigator of false
intelligence, 79–81
multilateralism, 6, 28,
114
Muravchik, Joshua, 6,
15, 57, 64, 69, 114
Muslims and Islam,
20, 62, 63, 70, 71–
74, 108–11, 175
Mylroie, Laurie, as
promoter of Iraq
war, 81
National Interest
magazine, 17, 113
National Review
magazine, 9, 106,
108

neoconservatism,
neoconservatives,
neocons, 13, 19,
107, *See also*
neoconservatives as
a force of persuasion
activities of, 5, 7,
57, 175–77
adherents of
exceptionalism,
14
and cohesion, 188–
93
and security of
Israel, 2, 10, 18,
55, 63, 67, 119–
20, 186
as a counterforce to
political realism,
17
as a persuasion, 17–
18
as Republican Party
members, 5, 213
aspirations of, 2, 6,
11, 58, 82, 83,
99, 105, 115,
118, 119, 121,
124, 154, 170,
175–77, 178,
181, 194, 199,
213
Dick Cheney and
kinship with,
152–56
growth out of
Trotskyite roots,
5
history of in US, 7,
17–18, 186–88
Norman Podhoretz
and, 17–18, 186–
88
OSP and, 35, 178,
181
relationship with
Israel's Likud
party and, 183
rhetorical study of,
1
strategy of praise,
98–99, 150–51,
189–91
*They Knew They
Were Right* book
(Heilbrunn) on,
192
unity of purpose,
29, 152, 188–93
welfare of Israel as
motivation for, 10

WMDs and, 2, 103,
124, 154, 181
"Neoconservatism in a
Nutshell" article
(Lobe), 55–57
neoconservatives as a
force of persuasion.
See also
neoconservatism,
neoconservatives,
neocons
beginnings
Albert J.
Wohlstetter
and, 1, 7, 11,
14, 15
as anti-Stalinists,
5
Cold War and, 5,
14
Henry M. Jackson
and, 1, 7, 15
Irving Kristol and,
2, 7, 17–18
Leo Strauss and,
1, 7, 8, 212
effectiveness, 2, 83,
84, 99, 118, 170,
188
cohesion, 188–93,
199–200

uses of think
tanks, 2, 57,
60, 187
Netanyahu, Benjamin,
Israeli Prime
Minister, 46, 67, 71,
115, 119, 120
New Republic
magazine, 27, 97,
106, 108, 114
New York Times, 26,
42, 58–59, 73, 85,
91, 97, 101, 103,
108, 117
A.M. Rosenthal, 85
apology, 80
as supporter of Iraq
invasion, 79–81
9/11. *See* September
11, 2001
Nixon, Richard M., 50,
140, 162
North Korea, 37, 177,
275
Novak, Robert, 42, 43
*Obsession-Radical
Islam's War against
the West*
documentary, 73–74
Office of Special Plans
(OSP)

as shadow
  intelligence
  agency, 178, 181–
  83
as vital mechanism
  in run-up to war,
  35, 182, 184, 201
indicators for
  success of, 184
producer of grist for
  the neocon mill,
  90, 178, 181, 184
rhetorical stylings
  of, 179
White House and,
  179
Operation Iraqi
  Freedom, 200
Oslo Accords, 32, 119
OSP. *See* Office of
  Special Plans
pathos, 91, 94
Pearl Harbor, and
  9/11 rhetorical
  equivalency to, 95,
  125, 165–66, 173
perception,
  management of, 3,
  83–90, 160, 201

Perle, Richard N., 20,
  22–29, 34, 40, 49,
  66, 69, 117, 152
as chair of Defense
  Policy Advisory
  Board, 24–27, 39,
  51, 158, 190
business
  involvements of,
  25, 26, 28
charges against, 26–
  27
coauthor of *A Clean
  Break*, 46, 71,
  119
Eleana Benador
  and, 85, 86
Henry M. Jackson
  and, 15, 23, 24,
  179
rhetorical manner
  of, 27–29, 52,
  170, 171
US presidents and,
  24, 113, 115,
  124, 130
Wolfowitz and, 15,
  19, 23, 29, 130,
  190–91, 212
Woolsey's rhetorical
  style vs., 52

Persian Gulf War, 20, 88, 114, 116, 125
persuasion, force of neoconservatism, 58, 87, 111, 166–72, 179, 207, *See also* suasion
consubstantiality in cohesion, 188–89, 192, 200–201
foreign policy and, 105
Irving Kristol and, 17–18
think tanks as tool in, 60, 201
use of media in, 84, 201
White House leadership and collusion with, 4, 200
Pipes, Daniel, 64, 73, 85
and "The Muslims Are Coming!" article, 109–10
as prolific writer and supporter of think tanks, 107–12

background and character, 61–63
media appearances, 62
MEF and, as founder, 61, 63, 107
MEMRI advisory board member, 71
rhetorical style of, 108–12
significant financial backing of, 111
son of Richard Pipes, 33
Pipes, Richard, Harvard professor and father to Daniel, 33, 187
PNAC. *See* Project for the New American Century
Podhoretz, John, son of Norman, 103
Podhoretz, Norman, 122, 187, 186–88, 191
as editor of *Commentary*

magazine, 17,
187
goal of
consubstantiality,
188
MEMRI advisory
board member,
71
on Jewish unity and
Zionism, 186
Powell, Colin, 78, 132,
277
preemption, advocacy
of
as contact in the
DPG, 117
as neocon strategy,
2, 6, 7, 59, 154,
209, 213
by Cheney, 149,
155, 214
Hanson, classicist
and historian,
146
Kissinger, 155
Wohlstetter, and, 12
Wolfowitz, 22
Project for the New
American Century
(PNAC), 104, 123–25

as advocate for Iraq
invasion, 165
founding statement,
121, 122, 142
membership, 31, 51,
96, 103, 121,
130, 180
origin and actions,
115, 121–26
Quayle, Dan, 46, 70,
102, 122
Rand Corporation, 11,
179
Reagan, Ronald, 20,
24, 30, 34, 36, 50,
53, 102, 179
and welcoming
neoconservatives,
113–14, 213
realism in government,
vs. unilateralism
(idealism), 5–7, 17,
28, 114, 154
Rendon Group,
perception
management and,
87–90
rhetoric, use of, 52,
54, 71–73, 115, 118,
See also rhetorical

composition and
cohesiveness
and theory of, 168,
171
application of ethos,
logos, and
pathos, 91–95
as a focus of study
in addressing
issues, 1, 157,
168
basic law and theory
of, 171
consubstantiality as
essential goal in,
189
use of syllogism in
analysis, 167–71
rhetorical composition
and cohesiveness.
See also rhetoric,
use of
Cheney and, 143,
150–51
in persuasion, 17,
57, 179, 189
intragroup
identification of
neoconservatives
and, 189

Kagan and, 100,
165–74
Perle and, 171
Pipes and, 108–12
think tanks and, 60
use of in push for
Iraq invasion, 83,
91, 170, 179
rhetorical theory. *See*
rhetoric, use of
Rice, Condoleezza,
129, 130, 135
Robb-Silberman
inquiry, 207, 209
Rodman, Peter W., 57,
122, 124
Roosevelt, Franklin D.,
53, 95, 165, 166
Rubin, Michael, 57, 85
Rumsfeld, Donald, 71,
122, 124, 130, 148,
157–63, 213
as secretary of
defense, 132, 159
Cheney and, 3, 115,
140, 141, 146,
158, 162, 176
Feith and, 34
irascible
temperament,
162, 185, 285

speechmaking, 195
Saudi Arabia, 56, 88,
  200
Schmitt, Gary, 57, 180
Scowcroft, Brent, 6,
  129
Senate Intelligence
  Committee, 179,
  207
September 11, 2001
  (9/11), 28, 51, 52,
  70, 81, 181
  as catalyst of
    neoconservative
    agenda, 2, 95, 98,
    165, 174, 185,
    192, 201, 213
  Benador Associates
    and, 85
  Bush speeches
    regarding, 66,
    136, 164, 176
  Cheney on, 149, 154
  Kagan and, 98–100,
    165, 166, 173,
    174
  Pipes and, 107, 111
  Rendon Group and,
    88
  W. Kristol on, 98–
    100

Wolfowitz on, 21,
  29, 165
"Shock and Awe", 67,
  182, 201
Shulsky, Abram, 70,
  179–81, 192
  as OSP director,
    181–82
  finesse in
    reciprocity, 191
  Henry M. Jackson
    and, 15, 179
Soviets / Soviet Union,
  16, 18
  and Cold War, 5, 14,
    23, 213
  DPG on former
    territory of, 118
  Wohlstetter's
    "Delicate Balance
    of Terror" paper
    on, 23, 50
Spender, Stephen, 17
Strauss, Leo, 7–11, 33
  at U of Chicago, 1,
    9, 11, 19, 179,
    212
  inspirational spirit
    and founding of
    US

neoconservatism, 1, 7, 8, 14, 188

Straussians, 8, 11, 179, 181, 192, 213

suasion, 99, 214, *See also* persuasion, force of

neoconservative, *See also* Cheney, Richard B.:suasory

Sun newspaper, Chilcot summary, 281–83

Syria, 56, 106

Tenet, George, 41, 137

terrorism/terrorists, 7, 53–54, 62, 66, 81, 82, 87, 94–95, 98, 106, 108, 142, 154–56, 164, 170, 175–77, 181, 195–97, 205

"The Muslims Are Coming! The Muslims Are Coming!" article (Pipes), 109–10

think tanks activities in, 31, 38, 46, 51, 57, 60–61, 97, 180, 187, 192

American Enterprise Institute (AEI), 38, 46, 65–67, 141

Heritage Foundation, 31, 74

Hudson Institute, 31, 69, 180

in promotion of invasion of Iraq, 2, 83, 96, 103, 175, 179, 201

Jewish Institute for National Security Affairs (JINSA), 38, 51, 67–69

Middle East Forum (MEF), 46, 61–63, 107

other notable organizations, 31, 38, 46, 51, 74, 180

Project for the New American Century (PNAC), 31, 51, 96, 103, 121–26, 180

rhetorical uses in, 60
Washington Institute for Near East Policy (WINEP), 46, 51, 63–65
Time magazine, 108, 132
Times of London newspaper, 281, 283
Trireme Partners, 26
Trotskyite(s)/Trotskyism, 5, 213
Truman, Harry S., 53
Trump, Donald J., 36, 50
Tyranny's Ally book, by David Wurmser, 47–49, 126, 171
United Kingdom (UK)
as the US's chief ally, 204
Chilcot report out of, 206, 211, 271–84
costs of Iraq war to, 205, 211

United Nations, 36, 113, 125, 153, 195, 275
Vest, Jason, 16, 68
Vietnam War, 51, 127, 142, 149, 205
Wall Street Journal, 85, 97, 106, 108
Washington Institute for Near East Policy (WINEP), 46, 51, 63, 64
Washington Post, 42, 85, 94, 96, 108, 145, 165, 168
weapons of mass destruction (WMDs)
abandonment of by Iraq after Gulf War, 125
Bush ultimatum regarding, 196
Chilcot report on, 276, 280
claims of Saddam's possession of, 2, 42, 78, 89, 99, 123–24, 153–57, 181
Judith Miller's modus operandi

in reporting on,
79
push for removal of
through war, 104,
154, 155, 181
Weekly Standard
magazine, 27, 31,
93, 97, 98, 103,
108, 121
Whitaker, Brian,
Guardian columnist,
65, 72
White House. *See also*
administrative triad,
See also Bush-
Cheney-Rumsfeld
nationalist triad,
function of
Bush and Cheney
alliance, 145, 214
Bush-Cheney-
Rumsfeld, as
unified
nationalist triad,
3, 163, 207
Judith Miller and,
79
Wilson, Joseph, 42, 43
WINEP. *See*
Washington

Institute for Near
East Policy
Wohlstetter, Albert J.,
11–13
and "Delicate
Balance of Terror"
paper, 22
at U of Chicago, 2,
11, 13, 75
Henry M. Jackson
and, 14
Perle and, 22–23,
117
Wolfowitz and, 19,
20
young neocons and,
7, 13, 14, 15, 131
Wolfowitz, Paul, 19–22,
29, 38, 66, 137,
152, 179
as deputy secretary
of defense, 21,
29, 34, 76, 115,
146, 158, 181,
190–91, 212
Distinguished
Service Award
winner, 17
finesse in
reciprocity, 191

G.H.W. Bush, 20,
116
Leo Strauss and, 1
on invasion of Iraq,
21–22, 29, 161,
165, 181, 200
Perle and, 15, 23,
29, 130, 190–91,
212
PNAC and, 122, 124
rhetorical style vs.
Woolsey's style,
52
Woolsey, Robert
James, 49–57, 64,
69, 71, 85, 86, 124,
165, 212
his "World War IV"
speech, 52–54, 56
rhetorical style vs.
colleagues', 52–56

World Trade Center
bombing, 81, 141
Wurmser, David, 46–
49, 56, 66
coauthor of *A Clean
Break* report, 47,
71, 119
Tyranny's Ally, 47–
49, 126, 171
Woolsey's rhetorical
style vs., 52
Wurmser, Meyrav, 56,
70–74, 85
coauthor of *A Clean
Break* report, 47,
71, 119
MEMRI and, 71–73
Zakheim, Dov, 58, 130
Zionism/Zionist(s), 8,
186–87
Zoellick, Robert B., 57,
124, 130, 168

About the Author *(by way of a brief eulogy)*

Let us praise a schoolteacher, Earl F. Osborn, who, from Healdsburg High School in 1944, wrote a letter to me, Harold the author, then, a petty officer third class of the 142nd Seabee battalion on duty in the Philippine Islands. Mr. Osborn wrote, "I've been looking at the records here and see that you should go to college after the war is over." Never before had anyone suggested "college" to me. We were a family who never talked about such things. In my ignorance, that goal—whatever it meant—was far out of reach.

In the Navy, I heard of a terrific opportunity called the GI Bill for WW2 veterans and talked about it with my buddies. It was a chance to learn—at no cost! Guys like us could go to any college and get free tuition, plus books and lodging, FREE. What a deal! As the old guy on the farm used to say, Get an education, son; that's something they can't take away from you."

This veteran "ate it up"—and never stopped consuming, passionately. Such excitement was a new experience in life: reading and analyzing, writing and debating. Wow!

MA followed BA. Then came the PhD and university teaching, the hard work and joy: books and articles, fantastic sabbatical leaves, gratifying honors—the works. Thrills in the classroom and library. To teach is to learn.

Then came retirement, had to happen. Six years later and another book. The studying never stopped.

In 2015, living at Merrill Gardens in Seattle, a senior residence, this experienced and equipped scholar found out that the fire in the belly was still aglow, and the more he came to understand how the invasion of Iraq happened, the more he felt compelled to continue digging, to know the story. He decided to tell what he had learned, *to put some light on the subject.*

I wrote the book because I wanted readers to know how, on March 19, 2003, we chose violence. Judiciously, I chose every word printed here. It's as close as this human can get to reporting on how the invasion occurred—who and why.

So here we are. Thanks, Mr. Osborn, for your part in setting up a productive life and this report. I know I'm a lucky man.

Made in the USA
Lexington, KY
04 July 2019